GLOB

*Tra*

# N...
# AND S...RENTO

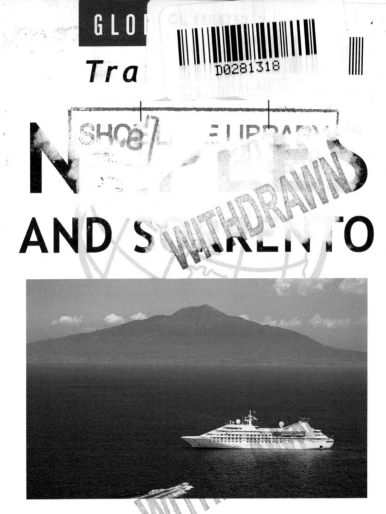

# MICHAEL LEECH &
# MELISSA SHALES

NEW
HOLLAND

NEW
HOLLAND

★★★ Highly recommended
★★ Recommended
★ See if you can

Fifth edition published in 2010
by New Holland Publishers (UK) Ltd
London • Cape Town • Sydney • Auckland

10 9 8 7 6 5 4 3 2 1

website: www.newhollandpublishers.com

Garfield House, 86 Edgware Road
London W2 2EA, United Kingdom

80 McKenzie Street, C
8001, South Africa

Unit 1, 66 Gibbes Stre
Chatswood, NSW 206

218 Lake Road, North
Auckland, New Zealar

Distributed in the USA
The Globe Pequot Pres

Copyright © 2010 in t
Melissa Shales
Copyright © 2010 in m
Copyright © 2010 in p
Individual photograph
Copyright © 2010 Nev

please share it with us by writing to the Publishing
Manager, Globetrotter, at the office nearest to you
(addresses on this page). The most significant contribution
to each new edition will receive a free copy of the
updated guide.

**Publishing Manager:** Thea Grobbelaar
**DTP Cartographic Manager:** Genené Hart
**Editors:** Thea Grobbelaar, Carla Zietsman, Melany McCallum,
Tarryn Berry

Creamer
Colleen Abrahams
Elaine Fick,

ape Town
ln. Bhd.,

pp. 35, 74, 114;
co: pp. 18, 30, 70;
ies: pp. 41, 85;
p. 11;

110;
iive: pp. 56, 57;

;

i8, 60, 76;
ge, pp. 4, 12, 16,
92, 95, 100, 117,

118;
**Richard Sale:** pp. 88, 98, 105, 106, 107, 108, 109;
**Melissa Shales:** pp. 20, 24, 38, 78, 81, 83;
*(HL: Hutchison Library; IP: International Photobank)*

**Acknowledgements:**
Melissa Shales would like to thank the following
for their help in researching this book: Go Airline;
Alessandra Smith and Michela Moguolo of the Italian
Tourist Office in London for their assistance in planning
the trip; Interhome holiday apartments; Royal-Continental
Hotel, Naples; Grand Hotel Royal, Sorrento; Excelsior
Vittoria Hotel, Sorrento; and Casa Albertina Hotel,
Positano for assistance with accommodation; Stephen
Fowler, as always, for his invaluable assistance with
research; the staff and patients of Nuovi Pellegrini
Hospital, Michael Burgoyne and Rosalba Viggiani of the
British Consulate in Naples for their help.

**Front Cover:** *Sorrento Fishing Harbour, Bay Of Naples.*
**Title Page:** *Vesuvius is the most densely populated volcanic region in the world.*

# CONTENTS

# 1
# Introducing Naples and Sorrento

Naples resounds to a drum roll of history. For thousands of years, it has led a double life – enjoying a privileged position beside the Mediterranean, yet in the dangerous proximity of a huge volcano. Throughout recorded history, **Vesuvius** has had long periods of calm, then sudden, often very violent eruptions. The most famous was in AD79 when a cataclysmic explosion sent magma boiling over and superheated air to bury **Pompeii** and **Herculaneum**. Reading contemporary descriptions still chills, and you can see in the now peaceful countryside the recovered ruins of its lost Roman cities.

The history of Naples is different to that of northern Italy – part of the southern kingdom of Naples and the Two Sicilies, retaining links with ancient Byzantium and with Bourbon Spain, driven always by maritime trade. Only when Italy was unified in the 19th century did this powerful city lose its status and its way. Easily walked, it has endless treats for those who are prepared to search beyond its dodgy reputation for grime and crime. Both still exist in its narrow alleys but it also has grand palaces and promenades, magnificent castles and gaudily decorative churches, and an elegant beauty that is only more poignant because of the graffiti-laden counterpoint.

Surrounding the city of Parthenope is the beautiful province of **Campania**, with some of the most famous sights in the world including the **Amalfi Drive** and the **Bay of Naples**, **Capri** and the vast royal palace of **Caserta**. There are numerous sites from antiquity too, and for those who like the simple life, exploration of

### TOP ATTRACTIONS

**★★★ Pompeii and Herculaneum:** freed from deep volcanic deposits, these towns are revealed again.
**★★★ Capri:** one of the most beautiful islands in the world.
**★★★ The Amalfi Drive:** cliffs, sparkling sea, vine framed villages and fishing boats seen from a shore-hugging road.
**★★ Old Naples:** a fascinating tangle, crowded and cheerful.
**★★ Sorrento:** a perfect little resort town looking across to Capri from its cliff-top perch.
**★★ Vesuvius:** visit the summit of this amazing live volcano.

**Opposite:** *Sorrento, ranged along its clifftop, overlooks the sea.*

## A LAYER CAKE

It is easier to imagine the underlying **strata** of Campania if you think of it as a gigantic cake. Growing on the surface is greenery, rooted in rich volcanic soil, brilliant subtropical growth on the top layer, which is white limestone, like a pale angel cake on the chocolate of the reddish brown **volcanic layers**. Deep down along the wide crescent of land surrounding Naples, the limestone itself is often thickly overlaid with solidified rock from eruptions, layers of lava, or dark, tightly compressed volcanic dust and cinder.

Campania's rich countryside and villages is recommended for extended drives, walks and visits. Naples has been catering for tourists for centuries, and now relieved of most of its dark images, it is even more alluring and easier to visit.

## THE LAND

The entire west-facing coastal area of Campania faces and slopes toward the sea, quite steeply at first from inland heights, then softening down to coastal hills. The stern backbone of the **Appenine Range**, the central mountainous spine running the length of Italy, rises to the east like a protective wall. Effectively creating markedly different east and west regions, it strides down from east of Genoa to Sicily. These often snow-topped mountains are of limestone, and near the south of Naples they are subject to earthquakes and volcanic eruptions due to volatile tectonic plate movements. The other principal heights are volcanic. The original substructure and the later volcanic activity of the area results in richly varied scenery.

Limestone forms the lower arm of the two promontories of land that enclose the famous **Bay of Naples**. The bay is a vast saucer of shielded water, a natural harbour. Sculpted into rugged shapes, it is also deeply cut and carved, and under the surface are large limestone caverns, some flooded. Along the coasts, the rock is indented by the sea and makes for a series of world-famous sights in a ravishing parade of capes, bays, and steep cliffs, some embraced with precipitous small settlements. At the foot are tiny beaches, backed by the soft azure of the Mediterranean.

**Below:** *The busy port city of Salerno is a good base for exploring the sites along the Amalfi coast and the Greek city of Paestum.*

## The Volcanic Origins of Campania

The area has always floated on a vast sea of hidden volcanic lava, the **Campi Flegrei**. Towering over it, Mount Vesuvius is really just a colossal relief valve that occasionally – and very violently sometimes – relieves in its eruptions the intense pressure building up just a few thousand metres below. The thick shielding layer of limestone caps the vast magma lake boiling below, and this is the foundation stone of Campania, lying at various depths beneath the whole province. Activity in the Campi Flegrei has been stronger since 2000, indicating new movements. The underlying superheated magma, relatively close to the surface, means the fostering and eruption of warm sulphurous springs too. These are found on the mainland and are particularly widespread on the island of Ischia.

**Vesuvius** is one of the most famous volcanoes in the world – dangerous, yet in repose extremely beautiful. The volcano has attracted tourists here for centuries with its infrequent yet often terrifying eruptions. Smoke still hangs lazily above Vesuvius, a warning that the fiery lady may appear quiescent, but is really only sleeping.

The lava, ash and dust fallen to earth from many ancient volcanic eruptions has richly coloured the Campanian soil and fertilized it well over many centuries. This, with the caressing warmth of the climate, has resulted in a mass of vegetation that is lush and green, even in the winter period. Indeed, this rural part of Italy will appeal to those who like to get off the track and explore. You can find here a natural Campania that has altered little, with unchanging hill towns, tiny villages, sometimes tumbledown and impoverished, and farms.

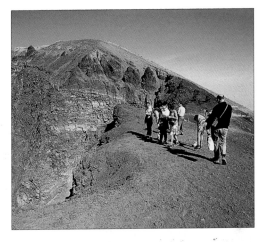

**Above:** *Tourists visiting Mount Vesuvius feel a great respect for this famous volcano, which could erupt at any time.*

### HIDDEN HELLFIRE

Volcanic action always marks the landscape and life of the region, even if many of the actual fires are long dead, leaving ancient **caldera**. *Campi Flegrei* means 'field of fire', and while this long concealed oven stretching beneath Naples and Cuma is no longer visible, it still makes its presence felt in small **earthquakes** and the many volcanic features of the area. Aside from **hot springs**, it provides spas for bathing in the sulphurous waters and treatments using volcanic mud.

## WORLD HERITAGE SITES

The area covered by this book is effectively one vast UNESCO World Heritage site – places listed include the historic centre of Naples; the 18th-century Royal Palace at Caserta with the Park, the Aqueduct of Vanvitelli, and the San Leucio Complex; the archaeological areas of Pompei, Herculaneum, and Torre Annunziata; the Amalfi Coast; and Cilento and Vallo di Diano National Park, which includes the archaeological sites of Paestum and Velia, and the Certosa di Padula.

## OLD LIVES REVEALED

Social life, both ancient and recent, is ever present in Campania. From the long buried mysteries preserved, and now exposed, at many excavated antique sites, principally Pompeii, to museums and spectacular Greek temples – this is a part of Italy that perpetually fascinates. Sites are well indicated and there are spacious car parks often with information and displays showing the background and facts on individual sites.

## Facts and Figures

**Campania**, one of Italy's smaller provinces, is 13,600 km$^2$ (5250 sq miles) in area. Yet it has in **Naples**, one of Italy's major cities, a population of around 800,000 (some 1.8 million if you include the whole Bay of Naples area). The province is not large, yet it is the second most densely populated area in Italy after Lombardy and the Milan conurbation.

Naples is the second biggest working port in Italy after Genoa, further north in Liguria. The port provides much local employment. It is centrally placed and you can actually drive through it as you enter Naples from the airport and see some of the activity. Or you can go to the quays by the rail station in the city to see it at first hand, though take care in this area. Otherwise principal industries are food production and export, (the pasta is notable) engineering, steel works and oil refineries.

The area is very important for its agriculture, with many products benefiting from an early, warm spring. Everyday and exotic fruits predominate, but in its sheltered valleys Campania grows a vast array of vegetables, fruits, nuts, olives, cereals and hemp. A most important industry is that of wine making, and the growing and cultivation of grapes has a very long and important history here. It is depicted in many ways, even, and notably, in frescoes from buried Pompeii. The wine is distinctive with a tang, some say, of volcanic vapours. Tobacco is also grown here – like France, Italy still has a large number of smokers.

Tourism provides a critical income, and there is a good infrastructure especially in the popular areas of Sorrento and the islands, including fair transport by train and road. There are first class restaurants and luxurious hotels of international aspect, some having helicopter terminals. Mount Vesuvius is the highest point at 1281m (4163ft).

## Climate

Campania is rarely too hot, and equally, not often cold. Although, it can be quite cool out of the hot months of summer, and even wintry in the eastern hills. At times, however, a sudden chill can descend and cause dank days early in the year. The city itself can be humid, especially in high summer, but breezes from the Mediterranean usually compensate. Rainfall is low.

Afraid you will find Naples too cloying and warm in summer? If the idea of staying in a city during hot periods is not to your taste, consider fresh air at nearby coastal towns, or even go inland. Possibilities (aside from the islands and other scenic areas) are Capua, Salerno, Avellino or Sorrento, which have easy access not only to Naples (a good train system operates) but to the local countryside too.

## The Coast

Italy has a coastline more than 7500km (4661 miles) long. The coast of Campania is only a small section of this very long shore which faces four seas – here it is the **Tyrrhenian Sea**. Along with eruptions, and the danger of earthquakes (the last in 1980), the Campanian coast has during all its history been constantly shaped, altered and added to by geological tremors. The stone you will see most of is the white chalky limestone, visible away from the volcano. Successive lava flows have covered it in

**MYTHS OF THE MOUNTAINS**

The ancient world looked on the **Bay of Naples** with a special respect. So famous was the beauty and mysterious aspect of the area, allied with the ferocious and unpredictable power of the living volcano, that in Classical times it was considered to be a mystical location. The **Lago d'Averno** is really a flooded crater, and its waters are particularly dark, lonely and atmospheric. Birds flying over were often asphyxiated by fumes, and thus it was regarded by both Homer and Virgil as the actual **mouth of the Underworld.**

**Left:** *The autostrada runs from Naples to the South, passing the outskirts of Salerno.*

**Below:** *The picturesque Amalfi coast is a popular tourist spot.*

the vicinity of the mountain, elsewhere it is often worn down by the elements. When it pokes through the green covering of the land, it is like glimpsing the submerged stony skeleton of Campania. Extending west of Naples and forming the edges of the large bite of the Bay of Naples, are two rocky arms of land. Once long peninsulas pointing into the **Mediterranean**, they are now broken at their ends into the islands of Prócida and Ischia to the north, both of volcanic origin, and Capri to the south. Together these two sea-girt extensions of Campania offer the best resorts and form the most famous scenic spots in the whole of Italy.

To the northwest of Naples the coast runs below Capua and Caserta in the hills above, the coastal road passing several seaside towns. This coastline extends to Sessa and the border with the neighbouring province of Lazio. A much longer stretch of coast runs southeast of the Amalfi coast, starting at Salerno and passing through Paestum, then Agropoli. From this town a secondary road runs south and then east by the sea, going through a number of small resorts and past rocky capes and headlands until it arrives at the province of Basilicata at Sapri.

## Flora and Fauna

The geography and vegetation of this warm world is attractive as a habitat to many birds and animals. **Lizards** and insects proliferate in the heat. The balmy climate and plenty of sunshine means **exotic plants**. Everywhere ancient **olive trees** cling to the soil, roots clambering over dry rocks, and although some of the trees are extremely old they still produce a much valued olive crop. It is certainly worth bringing a bottle back.

**Above:** *Olive trees, many of them hundreds of years old, thrive in the region's dusty volcanic ground, their luscious green and gold oil as carefully labelled as the finest wines.*

Beyond the industrial fringes and developed areas there is a great deal of wildlife, for this is a province dominated by plenty of open space. Hills were once heavily wooded, but became denuded as wood was used for industry and building. A programme of replanting has resulted in a return of trees over up to 25 per cent of the area. Although some plants here are imported species (the Australian eucalyptus, for example), there are many original plants.

Tree species found here include **pines**, **beeches**, **almond** and **citrus**, with many luxuriant **shrubs** from arbutus and juniper to acanthus and myrtle.

As with any countryside pursuit, you may need to bide your time and remain quiet in order to see local fauna. They include **foxes**, **rabbits**, **squirrels** and even **wild boar**. You will be lucky indeed to see the shy and rare **wildcat** and even shyer **wolf**, that still lurk in high and deserted mountain areas.

Many visitors only see the city and the coast, where **bird** life may be limited to doves, sparrows, or nimble swallows and the acrobatic swifts soaring over the rooftops of Naples. As the evening progresses small bats emerge to flitter over the towns. Among the many birds,

### BIRDS IN CAGES

Even in town centres you will hear and see bird life. Birds are popular **pets**, bred or captured, and are often seen (and heard) from their cages or on balconies. All over Italy small birds are also often used for **food**. Don't be surprised if you see skewered larks and thrushes on sale in the markets, or are offered them in restaurants, sometimes straddled over polenta as a local delicacy.

**Below:** *One of the many quaint fishing villages to be found in the Sorrento area.*

look for hawks, owls and along the coast and in the country, numerous warblers and finches. Stars among singing birds are blue rock thrushes and nightingales.

Bird watchers might consider a trip to the north, just across the border into Lazio. Here is the **Parco Nazionale dei Circeo**. Named after the witch Circe, and the legend of Ulysses and his men turned into pigs, there are many water birds here. It is a coastal strip of a series of marshes and wetlands near Anzio, together with a large lake, the **lago di Sabaudia**.

On city approaches and along highways you will see roadside plant shops. Like all Italians, Neapolitans love to load their gardens and terraces with blooming plants, vines, shrubs, even trees. Aside from many unusual sun-loving flowers and vines, you will also see on sale a vast variety of often beautiful terra cotta pots to plant them in, as well as sentimental sculptures. These are often sold at bargain prices, but if tempted to buy, remember they are heavy to transport home.

Italians are still fond of using fur for garments, and aside from being expensive they can also be high fashion, so don't be too surprised if you see women draped in furs, sometimes from exotic species. (Men too may sport fur collars or hats.)

# HISTORY IN BRIEF

With its many attractive aspects the area was a favoured place to settle even in prerecorded times. Hunters and gatherers were probably attracted by its natural geography – an easily accessible and extensive coastline with islands, and a defendable interior of hills and valleys. From ancient times it was home to Mediterranean peoples and prehistory offers a rich panoply of occupation.

Later, in a kind of ancient ribbon development, the coast received many settlers in antiquity, the shore becoming populated with small fishing and trading ports, settlements, religious buildings and villas. Up in the hills, small valley farms and the then vast woodlands provided a living for a tough hard-living peasant stock.

The natural beauty of the place was probably the last thing that drew original settlers. It was easy to get to by – water offered riches, fertile land and there was also the   sea's produce. In ancient times **Greece** and

## HISTORICAL CALENDAR

**Before 1000BC** Settlers live in the hills and many of the caves.
**600BC** Greeks from Cumae found Neapolis.
**146BC** Rome dominates for the next 500 years.
**AD79** Major eruption of Vesuvius which causes the destruction of Roman cities near the volcano.
**AD400** Slow establishment of the new Christian religion.
**AD555–600** Byzantine rule
**AD763** Naples becomes independent duchy.
**1139–1194** Normans rule
**1194–1269** Hohenstaufen Dynasty rules.
**AD1266–1422** Naples becomes part of Angevin kingdom, under Charles I.

**1269** King Conradin beheaded.
**1443** Alfonso I of Aragon enters, Naples colony of Spain for next 300 years.
**1631** Vesuvius erupts.
**1656** The plague kills thousands of people.
**1734** Arrival of Charles of Bourbon.
**1860** Unification of Italy.
**1870s** Outbreak of cholera.
**1922** Fascists in Italy
**1943** The Germans expelled from Naples.
**1944** Another major eruption of Mount Vesuvius.
**1950–60s** The *Cassa per il Mezzogiorno* scheme to protect historic old town.
**1980** Further eruptions of Mount Vesuvius.

**1987** Naples wins the football championship.
**1994** The G7 Summit opens in July in the city.
**1995** Historic Centre of Naples given UNESCO World Heritage Status.
**Late 1990s** Naples begins to show a new face – cleaner, safer and a good deal more crime-free.
**2002** With most of the EU countries, Italy joins the euro, now the national currency.
**2005** The new subway system, with its elegant decor, continues opening new stations along two lines.
**2007–08** Dispute over rubbish removal leaves the city wallowing in rubbish for months on end.

## GREEK SETTLERS

The **southern** the Italian peninsula was an integral part of the ancient Greek world. Long before the Romans, the Greeks had spread out from the mother country and explored their inland sea. They **colonized Sicily** and in **Campania** the coastal towns of **Paestum**, **Cuma** and **Pozzuoli** are but three settlements of Greek origin. Greek colonization affected much of this coastline and early towns were used as **trading links** establishing a policy of creating settlements over much of the Mediterranean world.

**Below:** *The Amalfi Coast, one of the most famous scenes in Italy.*

**Carthage** vied for power in the enclosed world of the Mediterranean. The first recorded arrivals were the Greeks, and those curious and very civilized people who spread down from the North and Tuscany, the Etruscans. They have all left their marks. The explorers settled around Sicily and all along the Southern Italian coast, founding trading posts and harbours. Examples of their fine and impressive architecture can still be seen. They put down roots, and it is often said that Neapolitans today still have a dark, Greekish look. Indeed Greek was the common language until the end of the Roman Empire.

Rivals for power, Greece and Macedonia were finally overpowered and subjected to Rome in 146BC. Rome from then on dominated ancient Campania for more than five centuries, bringing a new life to the area. Even 2000 years ago the balmy climate meant that this area was a lure for settlers and even early tourists. Towns along the sea were usually ports, but some seem to have been special places built in particularly attractive spots for relaxation and pleasure. Certainly after detailed excavation, social life in Pompeii was revealed as being on a grand scale with a huge arena for entertainment. Many inhabitants owned numerous luxuries in their houses and gardens, placed closely together along the narrow streets.

**Left:** *Pompeii viewed from the air, showing narrow streets.*

In the early Roman period several emperors, from **Tiberius** to **Nero**, attached themselves to Naples and its countryside. These two emperors were particularly renowned for their cruelty and venality, and Tiberius so enjoyed Capri life he actually governed the empire from there at the end of his life. Augustus lived in Ischia, later moving to Capri where his villa can be seen. Courts followed the emperors, Roman aristocrats built fine villas and well planned towns. As a rich and productive coastal region and part of the Mediterranean offering an alluring life, Campania has attracted many important settlers over the centuries.

Like much of the rest of Europe the medieval period was a time of consolidation and the gradual ascendancy of the Christian church. After the first millenium passed, the desirability of attaching this beautiful part of the world to their possessions attracted

### MAJESTIC MONARCHS

The principal rulers of the royal days of Naples are depicted in **niches** in the great palace in the centre of Naples. In actual fact, these niches were created by the need to shore up the palace which was foundering due to the many underground passages and caves below the city. The architect cleverly filled alternate spaces with supporting brickwork and stood **statues** in them. It is said they tell a story in a very Neapolitan style. Their grimaces and gesticulations, supposedly point to the fact that one king has commited à *faux pas.*

**Above:** *Piazza del Plebiscito is a huge pedestrianized parade ground, laid out in 1810.*

the leaders of other European countries. Foreign forces have always played a continuous part in the forming of Campania, particularly the French. After the Normans penetrated from the north and set up aristocratic courts in Sicily, as well as Naples, they made their main base at the preferred Palermo. By 1302, within 40 years of Charles of Anjou becoming King of Sicily, the **Angevins** had established a court in Naples. Their domain became known as, '**The Kingdom of the Two Sicilies**'.

Several aristocratic families have held sway here after the early incursions of the **Normans** from France. First the Hohenstaufens, then the Angevins (from Anjou), the Arogonese, the Spanish and eventually the French again, both Bourbons and Murats. During the 16th century, both Spain and France struggled for European domination, and for an extended time the French ruled in Campania. First the **Bourbons** ruled, but were later deposed after the Revolution and replaced by Napoleon's family, the **Murats** (who promoted good government).

During the 18th century, elegance flowered and the affluence of the aristocracy under the Bourbon family resulted in a good deal of building. Most evident is the royal palace at Caserta, up in the cool hills to the north of Naples. Caserta was designed to puff up the importance of the French style and taste, but Naples itself benefited enormously from the domination of the ruling family. The royal palace and the vast San Carlo Opera House in Naples, as well as many churches, are the monuments the era has left for us to enjoy. As the turbulent 18th century faded, the resilient Bourbons were reinstated after 1815. Indeed the family survived the upheavals of revolts to continue here until 1860. The final flowering of the old rule was artistic encouragement during the neoclassical era when the fine open Piazza del Plebiscito was created. The grand square with its Classical colonnade before a church was modelled on Rome's Pantheon. It has now been cleared of parked cars and can be seen as a glorious public space once again, although it seems more suited to be the approach of a government hall than a church.

Royal rule was finally severed after 1860 with the arrival of **Garibaldi's armies**. Intent on the unification of Italy and the joining together of the widely differing North and the South, the general was greeted as a saviour. Intent on pulling the Italian 'boot' right up to the Alps, and the establishment of a republic for the whole of the country, the Red Shirts swept up from the south. For the first time since the Romans, Italy was a complete country and not a series of separated states.

> ### SIR WILLIAM HAMILTON'S FINDS
>
> A devotee of Classical antiquity, **Sir William Hamilton** arrived in Naples in the late 18th century with his famous wife, Emma, who met Admiral Horatio Nelson here. Hamilton organized and financed several successful **excavations** around this time. There were many important finds, and Hamilton's people unearthed hundreds of artefacts at ancient sites, from **jewellery** to **armour**, and magnificent **kraters**, to **sculptures** and **vases**. Many can be seen in the fabulous collection at the Museum of Archaeology in Naples, others are displayed in the British Museum.

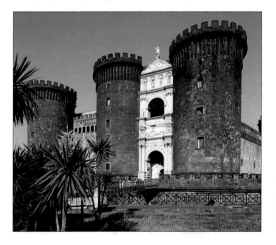

**Left:** *Castel Nuovo has an entry of sculpted white marble executed in the Renaissance style.*

## THE MINIATURE FRENCH REPUBLIC

When the **Revolution** rocked France, beheaded its Bourbon king and many aristocrats, scaring much of Europe, Naples had particular reason to fear reprisal. The city was governed by a branch of the **Bourbon family** and received emigrants such as the daughters of Louis XV. The Revolution brought a new government to Paris, and soon French troops arrived in Naples. In honour of the name Parthenope, the revolutionary (and Classically minded) French set up a **Parthenopaean Republic** until Napoleon's brother became king in 1806.

## THE EASY LIFE

Rather like the south of France, the coast here has always attracted **luxury lovers** and there are many **opulent seaside villas** by the shore and inland. They have been built here for over 2000 years, for the ancient (and rich) Romans enjoyed these **warm sea airs** and **scenic splendours** as much as we do today. Many of their seaside villas, often now fully excavated, are open to view, reflecting a very comfortable life. Some of these coastal places were actually holiday and retirement settlements 2000 years ago!

After the hail of events that accompanied the unification of Italy during the 1860s, Naples and its satellite towns began to suffer a series of economic hardships. The poor countryside and signs of depression still lingering today reflect the fact that Naples had a very definite boom and bust period – one from which it has only recently begun to emerge. After the establishment of the new complete Italy, the power of the one time rich city-state dwindled. Naples now had to compete with other Italian cities, and the population (particularly of its small towns) shrivelled as the agricultural economy no longer flourished. A deep, slow economical depression began.

Naples had been strong and powerful as a self-controlling unit but during the remainder of the 19th century and into the next, many problems appeared. The industrial base that had been built up was soon forfeited to the wealthy North, with its easier access to the rest of Europe. An economic slide began, resulting in poverty and eventually a crime-ridden town. You can see how the failing economy affected country towns when you tour the area. Many are ghosts of what they once were, reached by badly maintained roads and with antiquated buildings. This 'unspoilt state' can be a big bonus for tourism of course, for the towns, often clustered around a castle or a cathedral, can be very appealing. Dependent still on the countryside and small businesses, they can offer simple charm.

# GOVERNMENT AND ECONOMY

There are five administrative districts within the relatively small province of Campania, the City of Naples being one of them. Each has its own administration and district seat for the elected body under a mayor, and each has, incidentally, its own tourist board.

**Above:** *The Italian national flag.*
**Opposite:** *A restaurant along the coast offers superb views of the marina and the Bay of Naples.*

Naples is governed by a mayor and council. They sit in the imposing Palazzo di S. Giacomo on the Municipio Square, facing the sea and the main rail station. Other government offices are in the neighbouring squares of the Plebiscito, Trente and Trieste. It has to be said that although diminished, crime still has a hand in the politics of the area. This is a city that does things its own way.

In 1993 a new mayor, Antonio Bassolino, began a series of much-needed reforms in the city, starting with a serious effort to curtail the criminal efforts of the Camorra, a centuries-old network of organized crime families similar to the Sicilian Mafia. He also instigated a massive clean-up and restoration of the city, sprucing up its churches, palaces, castles and museums. There was a huge amount to do. Not only had the city suffered badly from poverty since the unification of Italy, but volcanic tremors had wracked the buildings while heavy bombing during World War II had contributed further disastrous damage. Topping this off was a massive population expansion in the 1950s and 60s, leading to some disastrous suburban sprawl and a positive plague of graffiti.

Bassolino's efforts paid off for a while and Naples arose phoenix-like from the ashes, but in the last few years, a creeping squalor has begun to encroach again. In 2007–08, the city was held to ransom by the Camorra over rubbish removal and garbage piled up on the streets for months on end until Berlusconi stepped in and did a deal. It has also been badly hit by the recession and the cracks, once again, are beginning to show.

## FLOATING AROUND

It is always an adventure to **go by water** to an Italian town. Be it Venice or villages lining the lakes, you have lots of choice here. On the **Bay of Naples** you can take a variety of craft to hop along the coasts and between the islands. In high summer the sea and harbours are busy with **ferryboats**, **hydrofoils**, **private yachts** and **cruisers**. In addition cruise liners call at Naples and pause at **Capri**, **Ischia** and **Prócida**. The islands and towns such as **Sorrento** are all served by frequent and fast water services, easily reached by year-round ferry from Naples.

The principal Naples airport is Capodichino terminal
with increasing international links. Transport is good,
although some roads are poor beyond the sea shore connections, as so much of the province is mountainous.

## THE PEOPLE

The people of Naples and Catania are definitely southern
in style and looks. They tend to be short, solid, dark and
full of vitality. They are described as vivacious, yet they
live in a world of fantasy and superstition, not to say
magic, rendering them at times mournful and fatalistic.

As soon as you leave Rome behind, you enter the
warm south, and a very different feeling is obvious on
the narrow streets of Naples and its satellite towns.
Crowded and noisy with chaotic traffic, the capital is
like no other Italian city. Although the province and
Naples have had a long and difficult 100 year decline,
the forces that are changing the city are bringing in new
business and it is enlivening and enriching a town that
was once in a wretched state. Although much of Naples
still seems decrepit and dirty, the changes are far
reaching, and the effects ongoing.

It is a society that takes advantage of the climate and
loves the outdoors, be it street life in a city or sitting beside
a square and enjoying life as it goes by in a small town.
At ease and also at work, they enjoy and share a
theatricality that is nationally recognized. Neapolitans use

**Right:** *Graffiti is an
ancient Neapolitan art-
form, proudly displayed
at Pompeii and, in
updated form, in
central Naples.*

their voices in song, that's very true, but they are also born actors and mimics. Displayed in public spaces, in squares, churches and parks you can see a regular expression of this exuberant art, for which Neapolitans are justly famed. They use the voice all the time, sometimes flaring into passion, but add a language that is universal – that of the body. Feet, hands, fingers, heads, arms, shoulders, torsos are all employed, and used to great dramatic advantage here as people converse volubly, both vocally and physically.

**Above:** *Locals relaxing in Sorrento, enjoying the sunshine.*

## Sport and Recreation

You have plenty of opportunity here to see a range of sporting activities. There is **golf**, **tennis**, **horse racing** and plenty of unusual things too. Becoming a popular local sport is a fast and exciting ballgame. Known as *peyote* in South America, it uses the long handled stick with a basket for hurling a ball.

Of the spectator sports **football**, or *calcio*, as in so many Italian cities, is a real passion, its star players raised to the elevation of gods. Matches are attended by huge crowds. Not always a position to be envied as it is a career that often ends very early. You go up – and you come down. The biggest name here in Naples is probably the star player **Maradona**, who rose to a meteoric height in local adoration, and even had a pizza created for him at the height of his fame in the likeness of his

### FOLK EVENTS

**Song** and **Dance** are important here and there are many local festivities, even festivals. Often you can join in. The showy Neapolitan **costumes** are an integral part of the popular art, and even if you don't see actual presentations you can't avoid the strident, infectious and often sentimental **music**. It echoes out everywhere, from solitary players, strolling **bands** and **radio** programmes, adding to the gaiety of the place.

**Right:** *There are several elegant shops located on Via Toledo.*

large-eared face. Eventually he fell into a sad world of obesity and unsavoury habits after a sad decline.

Campania has been catering to tourists for many centuries, providing them with a range of services, pleasures and things to do and see. The **shopping** is now exemplary, on a par with any large Italian city, with a range of well designed clothes, table ware, ornaments, artefacts and art objects. In turn, the flow of money has been welcomed, and now that Naples has turned a corner and is losing its dark image of dirt and crime it should be alluring to even more visitors. Among useful pastimes in the region are the making and display of souvenirs. The famous cribs and carved figures are only one aspect of the souvenir business.

A major slice of the people in Campania is not composed of residents. Inevitably Naples and its beautiful coasts are an attraction to many Italians as well as foreign visitors. It is a burden that local people have to bear that most visitors will arrive by road, for not only Neapolitans love their **cars**. Every weekend, most especially in summer, the roads south from Rome are filled with cars heading to the beaches and bars of the many resorts here. A world problem of course, as in the affluent countries or Europe, inhabitants love to use their vehicles.

---

### SOUVENIRS

There is no lack of souvenirs here, and local people are industrious and ingenious at making all sorts of things for sale. The Neapolitans have a fanciful imagination and it is challenged by anything clever or amusing. You'll see many street stalls set up to sell **embroideries**, **trinkets** and **figurines**. Browse, but also check in local shops. Look for good souvenirs in the **museums**, and **palace shops** such as at Capodimonte and Caserta, or Portici, another Bourbon residence.

## The Arts

Naples is a theatrical city, renowned throughout Italy for its flamboyance. Small wonder that **dance**, **music** and **mime** are appreciated in settings that are often theatre sets themselves. Scaramouch, the foxy old man of the **Commedia dell'Arte**, was born here. Music, dance and opera are popular and you will find street singers and entertainers of many kinds. Italy is ever a musical country, and Naples particularly so. Its mellifluous, sentimental songs are very popular.

In a city where life seems a theatrical art there are many **theatres** and **cinemas**. One of the biggest **opera houses** in Italy is here in Naples. Built in 1737, remodelled in 1816, the Teatro San Carlo is among the most famous of all the places of entertainment in Italy. It is a truly regal opera house. It is unprepossessing outside, standing beside the Palazzo Reale and the monumental arcades of the Galleria Umberto. Within it is a different tale. This is a classic Italian house with five levels of boxes surrounding a pit before the stage, built as much for social pleasures as for art.

**Below:** *The magnificent interior of the Teatro San Carlo. Biggest in Italy, the huge red and gold opera and concert hall seats up to 3000 people, and has brilliant accoustics.*

## UNDERGROUND ART GALLERY

At one time the **Catacombs** of **San Gennaro**, north of the city, were a refuge from persecution for early residents of Campania. The extensive and large **galleries**, with **tombs** and a sculpted **basilica**, date from the 4th and 5th centuries. They are carved out of soft volcanic tufa and are spread over two levels. Aside from tomb paintings there are **frescoes** and **mosaics**.

**Below:** The Farnese Hercules at the Museo Archeologico Nazionale.

There is a regular opera and ballet season here, with visits from foreign companies too, and you can tour the theatre at certain times when it is not in performance or being used for rehearsals.

Undoubtedly one of the greatest attractions here is the vast **Museum of Archaeology** on the northern edge of the central city. Here many of the most important finds from the Classical sites around the city are to be found. Even if you are not intrigued with Roman and Greek history, you must not miss this museum. Housed in a 16th-century building are galleries of sculpture (Roman and Greek), mosaics and frescoes (many from Herculaneum and Pompeii) as well as numerous small bronzes, silver, ivory and glass along with simple kitchen utensils. Together they make up one of the most important museums in the world for Greek and Roman arts. There is also a gallery with items depicting the history of Naples. Unfortunately galleries can often be closed, so call ahead and be sure to ask about tourist tickets.

There are museums at the **Certosa di San Martino**, showing the famous 18th- and 19th-century Neapolitan cribs and figurines. And at the **Capodimonte Palace** the Pinacoteca holds some fine works from **Bellini** to **Correggio**, as well as works from outside Italy, including two rare **Breughels**. Also here are the Royal apartments with a display of porcelain. At the **Museo Madre**, a restored old town palazzo is the somewhat unlikely setting for an extraordinary collection of modern greats from Damien Hirst to Robert Rauschenberg and Andy Warhol. The contemporary art theme continues at **PAN** in Chaia.

## The Visual Arts

Early visitors were **Giotto**, **Simone Martini** and sculptors, some brought by **King Robert of Anjou**, who also drew Petrarch and Boccaccio to his city. There is a particular school of Neapolitan painting that flourished in the 17th and up to the 18th century, a vibrant time, whose main figure is the master **Caravaggio**. His followers include **Luca Giordano** and **Carraciolo**. You can see examples of this period at the city's galleries and in churches.

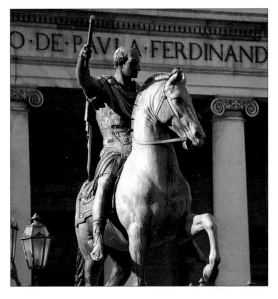

**Above:** *The statue of Charles III, by Antonio Canova, in the Piazza del Plebiscito.*

Unlike some other Italian provinces, however, you will not find many major artists in Campania. Rather there is a plethora of extraordinary decoration, particularly in the countryside with florid pictures and clever effects, anonymous sculptures in towns and in the churches, carved by local artisans who are often inventive craftsmen.

While the architecture of the city is unusual it is not unique in style. Yet many fine artists have worked here – **Fernando Sanfelice** was an architect with flamboyant tastes who created elegant courtyards with his trademark staircases as stellar features. **Luigi Vanvitelli** designed the Royal palace, and later the ponderous palace of Caserta. He was also a sculptor, while the great **Canova** carved statues (two are on the central Piazza Plebiscito). When you go into local churches, however, you will find plenty to look at – mostly exuberant local works, colourful yet more in the style of folk art.

### ANTIQUE CONNOISSEUR

Just to show that museums are not modern inventions, look at the the first floor gallery of the **Museo Archeologico** for the rooms dedicated to the **Villa di Pisone**, buried at Herculaeum. It probably belonged to a collector, who may have been related to **Julius Caesar**. In antiquity this was a private collection of extraordinary objects. They range from a series of statues to the priceless contents of a library of papyrus sheets.

**Above:** *The ornate Baroque interior of the Church of Gesù Nuovo. The church is situated in the long street also known as Spaccanapoli. See also Santa Chiara and its vast cloister.*

## Architecture

Naples has amazing buildings, none more extraordinary than a parade of high Baroque monuments that reach the heights of both interior and exterior decoration, very much to the gaudy Neapolitan taste. There are literally dozens of palaces and churches in the crowded streets and squares, the ornaments of this once splendid and affluent city. At last, after many decades of decay, these often over-the-top, yet splendid buildings are beginning to be cared for. If you are only able to visit one, make it the **Church of Gesù Nuovo** which was once a palace fronted with diamond-faced stones. (It is similar to the Palazzo dei Diamante in Ferrara.)

In the piazza before it is a theatrical monument, a tall Baroque column to the Virgin. Just along the street is a contrast – once overlaid with Baroque decoration the tall, high church of Santa Chiara was restored to its pure Provençal Gothic style after war-time bombing in 1943. In another contrast two formidable fortresses, the severe and sea girt **Castel dell'Ovo in Santa Lucia** of Norman origin and the impressive **Castel Nuovo** right in the city centre, are monumental examples of their era. The latter is also a marriage of styles, a 13th-century stronghold modelled on an example in the country of the then-rulers, far-off Anjou and the grand castle of Angers. It has an enchanting entry of sculpted white marble in the Renaissance manner. More contrasts? The main rail station squatting on the water front is an exercise in the bulky yet impressive 'Mussolini-esque' style of the late 1930s. Beside **Art Deco** examples, Naples also has **Art Nouveau** touches.

## Food and Drink

Agriculture has always been the key facet of the area beyond Naples. Despite the fact that over 80 per cent of the province is hilly or mountainous. No doubt about it, the food and **wine** of this fertile area is abundant, lush and delicious. The fields and terraces of the country produce a great variety of **vegetables** and tree-ripened **fruits** from the rich soils and constant sun. These include oranges, lemons, tangerines, figs, nectarines, apricots, peaches and melons, while asparagus and artichokes are early arrivals. The vines laced along their terraces are loaded with grapes in season for making wine, and also for the dessert dishes of the area. A range of local **cheeses** is found in the country. Ricotta and mozarella (from the buffalo) are often used in cooking. Plenty of **meats** too; try the dried and cured meats, raw and cooked ham and sausages. There are cakes and desserts that are unique to Campania which should definitely be sampled.

From the sea come huge harvests of **fish** and **crustacea**. The shellfish is amazingly varied. Markets, on the streets of the towns, show just how much harvest the sea produces. Not surprisingly one of the businesses of Naples is food processing.

**Below:** *Delicious Italian pizza served with salad.*

## FOOD TREATS

Even if you can't take back fresh fruits and meats, they are **preserved** and **cured** in many ways here, from **sausages** to smoked **hams**. Neapolitan **salami** comes in neat packages, is spicy and well fatted. Visit a grocery or supermarket to find tinned **vegetables** and preserved meats that are vacuum wrapped. Capri specializes in bottled fruits using local **liqueurs**. You can find **berries** in fruit liqueurs, **prunes** in anise, and sometimes **nuts** too. These expensive little jars are not always a luxury you may buy for yourself, but they make good gifts.

**Below:** The Pugliano Market in Ercolano, one of the many fruit and vegetable markets found in Naples.

Naples is internationally famous for two popular foodstuffs. The city has come up with at least two well-known dishes, which were first created here. One, the **pizza** was born in the back streets and can still be tasted in its original forms even in smart little restaurants. It is certainly to be found at its best here. Basically a flat pie made of tomato, cheese and additional garnishes decided by the cook, it is best baked in a brick oven, so that its special dough crisps on the hot floor, and it is still very much a local delicacy.

Even better known – and almost a symbol of Italy – is **spaghetti**. This is the local pasta form and now known around the world, available in Italian restaurants as far apart as Sydney and San Francisco. Spaghetti in long thin strands cooked to the correct *al dente* consistency then looped in deep plates, oiled or creamed, and married to a myriad sauces is definitely a Neapolitan dish. Here you can sample the authentic classic version. One of these is *con vongole*, or with little clams in their shells.

**The ancient olive** trees provide the deep golden oil that is the base of so many Italian dishes. You can also buy the **oil** to take home. Salad dishes are inventive and richly dressed.

Try eating **alfresco**. Lots of possibilities for picnics here – shop locally for all sorts of crusty breads, olives,

**Left:** *Bottles of Italian olive oil for sale.*

### EXOTIC DIGESTIFS

The many **herbs** that grow naturally here scent the air, and are much used in the local dishes. They may also be used in the many **liqueurs**, which are varied and made from fruits and nuts. **Strega**, a sweet yellow liqueur, is famous, but look for orange, mandarin, lemon, melon and various berry preparations, often presented in the most elegantly shaped and coloured bottles. Delicious in cocktails, after a meal, or simply as a stylish present.

nuts, cheeses, hams, olives and the tangy, locally produced salami. There are plenty of fresh vegetables, salads and fruits, and to drink try a local '*birra*' or **beer**, or fresh chilled white **wine** from the vineyards on the slopes of Vesuvius.

Vines have been carefully cultivated here for thousands of years, and wine of the locality was famed as long ago as the time of the Roman emperors. (Wine shops were excavated at Pompeii with sunken bowls in their stone counters as well as pottery containers.) Even in this generally dulcet Mediterranean clime they are cosseted, the tender shoots protected against possible winter chills with straw and rattan matting. In the ripening season grapes cluster along long lines of vines. Some are for eating but most are used for local wine production.

The wines that come from the terraces of the mountainside are much enjoyed. The long looping vines ranging high up the mountainside produce red wines from heavy bunches of grapes swollen from the volcanic soil they thrive in. Best know varieties are **Falerno** while Ischia produces white wines including the **Mount Epomeo** reds and whites. **Capri** has both red and white too, which can be sampled at small local inns. It is claimed that the wines of Campania benefit from a tinge of the volcanic sulphur in the subsoil in their bouquets.

### PASTA

Some claim that pasta is a Chinese invention, introduced to Italy by Marco Polo in the 12th century. This, emphatically, is not true. Pasta-making equipment and a half-eaten bowl of pasta and beans (still a local tradition) were found in the ruins of Pompeii. Naples was the great pasta centre of the 18th century, with 280 macaroni sellers by 1785. It was here that spaghetti was first conceived, although it lost its supremacy during the Mussolini era when the plains of the northwest were intensively planted with durum wheat.

# 2
# Naples

Naples has never been an ordinary city, but one that has lived at extremes of luxury, cruelty, poverty, beauty, indolence and fire. It was founded by the Greeks (Neapolis means 'new city'), ruled by the Romans, Byzantines, Normans, Spanish, French and, only belatedly, the Italians. Largely cut off from northern Italy, it has looked to the sea and developed a cosmopolitan feel. For centuries outsiders have described the people of Naples as being passionate, romantic and poetic or lazy, shiftless and untrustworthy. Whatever the reality, they arouse strong feelings in the outsider; not once has anyone claimed the city or its people to be boring.

The 20th century saw Naples decline abruptly, stripped of power by the unification of Italy. As poverty and neglect swept its streets, the city fully deserved its reputation as a den of crime. However, while not yet perfect, things have improved greatly in recent years and those who fall back on out of date clichés miss one of the most entertaining – and beautiful – cities on the Mediterranean.

Naples has an incomparable setting. Lord Byron rated it second only to Constantinople (Istanbul). Many of its buildings are crumbling, but they do so aesthetically, while others have benefited from a long overdue clean-up and restoration that has been helping to put the city in its rightful place on the European stage. It's difficult getting rid of the squalor, but with an incomparable setting, fine architecture, magnificent restaurants, great nightlife and a promenade perfectly designed for strolling, nothing will hold this city down forever.

### DON'T MISS

★★★ **Museo Archeologico Nazionale**: a great collection of Graeco-Roman art.
★★★ **Spaccanapoli**: this street is the last surviving relic of the ancient Greek grid plan.
★★★ **Porto di Santa Lucia**: the medieval **Castel dell'Ovo** surrounded by the Borgo Marinara (Fishermen's Quarter).
★★★ **Parco e Museo Nazionale di Capodimonte**: a beautiful palace, art collection and park.
★★ **Certosa di San Martino**: the best view out across Naples and the Bay.

**Opposite:** *The Galleria Umberto I with its impressive glass-dome roof.*

## NAPLES BY AREA

The best way to get your bearings is to look at Naples from the sea, with the city laid out in front of you like a map, each area ascending the last to reach the clifftop.

Naples is laid out along the northern section of a horseshoe bay. Along the northern arm (to your left) are the towns of **Pozzuoli**, built on a volcanic field, known as the **Campi Flegrei** (*see* page 53), and the elegant suburb of **Posillipo**. At the corner is the resort area of **Mergellina**. Beyond this, just to the left of the city centre, is the seaside walkway, the **Lungomare**, fronted by several of the city's finest hotels and definitely the place to stay. Just behind and above the Lungomare, **Chiaia**, an area first constructed by the Spanish in the 17th–18th centuries, is now one of the city's trendiest shopping and nightlife areas, filled with designer boutiques and bijou bistros.

Continuing up the cliff, the smart residential district of **Vomero** is wrapped around the vast **Castel Sant'Elmo**. Built mainly in the 19th century, the suburb cascades across the peak and down the far side of the ridge.

Directly below it, halfway down the cliff and largely concealed, is the *Centro Storico* (Historic Centre) – the original city centre. The area is generally considered to be bounded to the west by Via Toledo, to the north by Piazza Cavour, and to the east by Corso Garibaldi. To the south, it technically stretches down to the waterfront, but the boundary of the 'tourist' zone is marked by **Piazza Bovio** (former home of the Stock Exchange) and **Corso Umberto I**, built as a slum clearance project to connect the port and railway station in the early 20th century.

Back on the seafront, almost exactly at the centre of the bay, you come to the city's icon, the 12th-century **Castel dell'Ovo** (Castle of the Egg), and a little peninsula on which stands the traditional fishermen's quarter (Borgo Marinara) of **Santa Lucia**.

Historic Centre

Just to the right (south) of this are the city's main ferry port, and the Spanish royal city centre, dominated by the brooding bulk of the **Castel Nuovo** and the **Palazzo Reale**. The rest of the seafront is taken up by both naval and commercial dockyards. Just behind these, on Piazza Garibaldi, is the **Stazione Centrale**. This waterfront area with four high-rise apartment blocks is not a safe place.

Above them on the clifftop, the **Capodimonte** area is lush, green and peaceful with one of the city's best museums and several good hotels. Finally, continue south and you see the towering cone of **Mount Vesuvius** (see page 63), totally surrounded by poorer commuter suburbs. Amongst them is **Ercolano** (see page 65), built on the ruins of ancient Herculaneum.

**Right:** *The Museo Archeologico Nazionale has an extensive collection of ancient art.*

## SIGHTSEEING IN NAPLES
### Naples National Archaeological Museum (MANN)

The Museo Archeologico Nazionale di Napoli, although obviously short of funding, and needing redecoration for some of its many rooms, houses one of the greatest collections of Classical art and sculpture. They come from several important collections, including finds from Herculaneum (housed here since 1797); Pompeii; and the world-famous Farnese Collection, brought to Naples when Charles III Bourbon inherited it from his mother, Elizabeth Farnese in 1731.

As you enter, the ground floor is a tranquil marble world of **Graeco-Roman sculpture** including various gods and goddesses, sportsmen, politicians and sarcophagi. Amongst them is a fascinating set of portrait busts of Socrates, Euripides and, supposedly, Homer, along with various Roman emperors, and a 2nd-century AD statue of the many-breasted Artemis from Ephesus. However, the highlights both come from the Caracalla Baths in Rome – a superb statue of Hercules, all curly hair and rippling muscles, and the massive Farnese Bull, a complex, towering sculpture telling the legend of Dirce, who was tied to a bull and tortured by her stepsons, Ampheon and Zethus. Beyond, stairs lead down to the basement, and a fascinating collection of **Egyptian art** sadly overlooked here amongst the jewels of Pompeii.

Head up to the mezzanine floor and turn left for a dazzling array of **Pompeii mosaics**, of which the most important undoubtedly depicts Alexander the Great's epic victory over King Darius of Persia. To most visitors however, this pales beside the more domestic charms of the *Cave Canem* (beware of the dog) sign, the fighting cocks, the marine mosaic showing an octopus and lobster locked in conflict, or the simple picture of doves drinking from a bowl.

Across the hallway, to the right, the **Napoli Antica Gallery** houses a small display of the history of Naples, together with an interesting collection of ancient household utensils and some beautifully modelled votive terracotta heads.

Up on the first floor, turn left for a stunning collection of small bronzes, silver, glass and ivory from Pompeii and Herculaneum with elaborately decorated helmets and oil lamps and the magnificent glass Blue Vase – the inspiration for centuries of Wedgewood design. A partial reconstruction of the Temple of Isis helps to put many of the finds in this section into context before you arrive at the superb collection of frescoes from Pompeii,

**HORSES TO COURSES**

The building now housing the Archaeological Museum was originally commissioned in 1582 as the Royal Riding School, but the site proved unsuitable and a university was created here instead. Between 1701–35, it was used as barracks before being returned to the students until 1797, when it first became a museum, art school and studio, and national library. With more and more collections being added it began to bulge at the seams, and gradually various elements were moved out. By 1957, the museum had assumed its current form.

**SECRET MUSEUM**

Definitely for adults only, while in MANN, look out for the Secret Museum, the collection of erotic and, at times, downright pornographic material from Pompeii. Romans had a very different view of sexuality from the modern one and much of this material would have decorated public spaces such as dining rooms.

**Left:** *An excellent collection of frescoes has been unearthed in Pompeii.*

Map showing: MANN (Museo Archeologico Nazionale di Napoli), Via Enrico Pessina, Via Atri, Via Luciano Armann, Via Duomo, Duomo di San Gennaro, Accademia di Belle Arte, San Paolo Maggiore, Pio Monte della Misericordia, Cappella Pontano Santa, Via Tribunali, Piazza Bellini, San Lorenzo Maggiore, Porta d'Alba, Santa Maria del Purgatorio, San Gregorio Armeno, Piazza Dante, Via Nilo, Museo Civico Filangieri, Via Benedetto Croce

**Opposite:** *Porta d'Alba is one of the original city gates of Naples.*

Herculaneum, Stabia and Paestum. Many follow the familiar themes of ancient mythology, but there are also landscapes, portraits and trompe l'œil architectural studies, all still brilliantly fresh in colour and emotion.

The first room to the right of the main stairs is dedicated to the collection of the Roman antiquarian who lived in the Villa de Pisone, Herculaneum, amongst which was a priceless library of 800 parchments (photographs only on display). Perhaps even more awe-inspiring in the gem collection beyond is the Farnese Cup, probably carved in Ptolemaic Alexandria, as a giant, exquisite cameo.

### The *Centro Storico* (Historic Centre)

A short distance downhill from the Archaeological Museum, **Piazza Dante** was built by Charles III on the site of an old market. Its monumental columns at the back represent the virtues of the king, but his various autocratic poses and the 18th-century elegance of his design are perpetually troubled these days by the exhaust fumes of a hundred buses. At the back of the piazza, a small tunnel lined with bookshops leads through the **Porta d'Alba**, one of the original city gates, taking you instantly into a different world of tiny, dark alleys. A block in, pretty **Piazza Bellini** has a monument to the composer, Vincenzo Bellini and a variety of attractive cafés. Nearby is an 18th-century convent which now houses a fine collection of 19th-century paintings by local artists, the **Accademia di Belle Arte** (Academy of Fine Arts; Via Vincenzo Bellini 36). The piazza marks the start of Via Tribunali, the most northerly of three main east-west thoroughfares of the ancient Greek city (Decumani). Next block down is the second road, the famous Spaccanapoli; little remains of the third ancient road, to the south. There are quite a few fascinating churches along Via Tribulani, but conserve some strength and don't try to visit them all; the entire old town is crammed with churches and several are unmissable. Those on Via Tribulani include the Renaissance **Cappella Pontano**, Baroque **Santa Maria del Purgatorio**,

### Too Much to See

Although distances are not long, start early when exploring the *Centro Storico*. Not only are the churches incredibly thick on the ground, but most only open in the morning. The tourist office in Piazza del Gesù can provide a detailed map showing four historic walking itineraries around the old town, taking in most of the churches and palazzos, as well as the signposted Via dell'Arte.

the richly decorated Baroque **San Paolo Maggiore** which stands on the site of the ancient forum, next to one of the entrances to underground Naples (*see* page 44), and the magnificent medieval **San Lorenzo Maggiore**, built in 1265, although the interior is a feast of Baroque excess. It is here that Boccaccio is said to have first seen his muse, Fiammetta, while Petrarch lived next door. The cloister gives access to various archaeological excavations including the Roman macellum (marketplace). Last stop on the street is the **Pio Monte della Misericordia**, a 17th-century charitable institution for the poor and ill Christian slaves freed from the Ottomans. Amongst several fine paintings is an altarpiece by Caravaggio depicting *The Seven Works of Mercy*.

**MIRACLE BLOOD**

In AD305, under the reign of Diocletian, San Gennaro (St Januarius), the Bishop of Benevento, was martyred and taken to the catacombs of Naples for burial. En route, his blood liquified in the hands of St Severus, who had the foresight to save two phials. Since then, twice a year, in May and September, the miracle is repeated amidst great celebration. It is taken as an omen of good fortune for the city and the occasional no-show is greeted with prophesies of disaster.

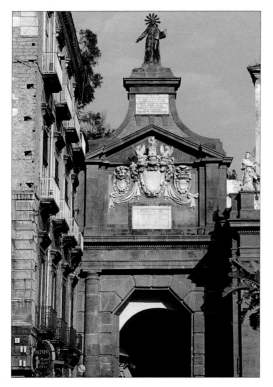

**MODERN ART MUSEUMS**

Three excellent museums in Naples all showcase contemporary art. **Madre** (Museo d'Arte Donna Regina, via Luigi Settembrini 79, tel: 081 1931 3016, www.museo madre.it) is a restored palazzo in the historic centre with a permanent exhibition tracing many of the greatest names in modern art from Roy Liechtenstein to Gilbert & George alongside regular exhibitions. The **Hermann Nitsch Museum** (vico lungo Pontecorvo 29/d, tel: 081 564 1655, www.museonitsch.org) is a converted power station given over to plastic arts. **PAN** (Palazzo delle Arti Napoli, via dei Mille 60, Chaia, tel: 081 795 8604/5, www.palazzoartinapoli.net) concentrates on temporary exhibitions only.

## THE GREAT DIVIDE

The Spaccanapoli is the most
famous street in Naples, but
you will never find its name
(meaning 'Naples-splitter')
on a map. The ramrod
straight thoroughfare that
bisects the old city is known
by various names along its
length. It is one of the few
surviving remnants of the
original ancient Greek city.
Parts of the old Greek city
walls have been excavated
in Piazza Bellini, on the
edge of the old town.

At the far end of the road, turn left for the **Duomo di
San Gennaro** (Cathedral of St Jannarius; Via Duomo
147), consecrated in 1315, but considerably altered
over the years – the Gothic façade actually belongs to
the late 19th century. The building is spacious and has
been well restored, with attractions from chapels with
good sculptures to that of the two phials of the blood of
San Gennaro, patron saint the city. There are frescoes
by Luca Giordano, and fine ancient mosaics in the
extraordinary underground basilica and baptistry of
**Santa Restituta**. There is a fee, but well worth it. The
monumental spire in Piazza Riario Sforza, the **Guglia
di San Gennaro** was erected to thank San Gennaro
for saving Naples from the eruption of 1631. A couple
of blocks down Via Duomo is a fine building that
has done duty as a late 15th-century palace and 16th-
century monastery and is now the **Museo Civico
Filangieri** (Filangieri Museum; Via Duomo), home to
the fine art collection of Prince Gaetano Filangieri.

Return to the Via Tribulani and turn left beside San
Lorenzo Maggiore onto **Via San Gregorio Armeno,**
Clustered along this little sidestreet are the workshops of

**Right:** *Long, straight
Spaccanapoli cuts
through the heart of old
Naples, and contains
some fantastic churches
and palazzos.*

many makers of *presepi* (Christmas cribs). The crafting of *presepi* is traditionally a family affair, with workshops handed down through the generations. Look very closely at the detail. At the centre you will find the Holy Family, but in addition to the traditional shepherds and wise men, you will find hundreds of other characters, from Turks to crippled beggars, musicians and the aristocracy.

Just off the street is the **Certosa di San Gregorio Armeno** (Monastery of St Gregory of Armenia), a real secret place. Enter up a ramp to find a garden and a convent founded in the 8th century by a group of nuns who fled the Iconoclasts in Byzantium to preserve the relics of St Gregory. Rebuilt during the 15th and 16th centuries with an elegant cloister, today, the interior is sumptuously decorated with a 16th-century gilded wood ceiling, two Baroque organs, and 18th-century frescoes by Luca Giordano.

## SPACCANAPOLI

Continue along Via San Gregorio Armeno and turn left onto Via San Biagio dei Librai, a treasure trove of antiques and handicrafts and the first stage on your tour of the famous Spaccanapoli. If it is open, make a quick stop at the impressively decorated Cappella dei Monte di Pietà, in the Palazzo Carafa, a charitable foundation built in 1597–1605 with a magnificent 18th-century sacristy. The entrance is flanked by sculptures by Pietro Bernini (1601).

As you continue down the street, look to your right for the **Largo Corpo di Napoli** (Body of Naples), an ancient Greek statue that has been adopted as one of the symbols of the city (*see* panel, page 39). On the other side of the road, the 15th-century **Church of Sant'Angelo a Nilo**, has a magnificent tomb sculpted by Donatello in 1426 and shipped down from Pisa. Its inhabitant is Cardinal Rinaldo Brancaccio, founder of the church, whose family palace stood next door.

The window-shopping gets more impressive as Naples becomes smart and affluent again. The **Piazza San Domenico Maggiore** has one of the most stylish cafés in the city, ideal for a break before delving back into the churches and the **Basilica di San Domenico**

## BUILDING THE NATIVITY

The *presepio* (Christmas crib) is one of Naples' most enduring art forms, first mentioned in 1025. Originally simple, they began to grow in scale and complexity from the 16th century onwards. The size of the scene is immaterial, from elaborate creations as large as a small room, depicting entire towns, to exquisite miniatures housed in an eggshell. Most are made of terracotta, but there are versions in wood, papier maché, plaster and even coral. The whole scene must be one not only of plenty, but severe over-indulgence, laden with tiny hams, pasta, cheese, bread, fruit and cakes. Today, people are again beginning to create modern dress figurines.

**Maggiore**. Originally built in 1238, there is little sign of its medieval origins in either its 16th-century exterior or 19th-century neo-Gothic interior. However, there are 45 Aragonese tombs, some 14th-century frescoes, probably by Pietro Cavallini, a pupil of Giotto, and a supposedly miraculous crucifix, which is said to have spoken to St Thomas Aquinas, who lived nearby. It can be found in the Capellone del Crocifisso.

Just behind the church, an alley on the right leads to one of the highlights of the old city, the charming little **Cappella Sansevero** (Sansevero Chapel; Via de Sancti) built as the Sangro family funeral chapel in 1590. It has some fine frescoes and paintings, but these are put in the shade by three cunningly carved statues – *Chastity* (a veiled woman) and *Despair* (a man struggling with a net), to either side of the altar, and a *Veiled Christ* by Guiseppe Sammartino in the centre. They may not be high art, but they are indeed impressive. Prince Raimondo de Sangro, responsible for remodelling the chapel in 1749–71, was a legendary character who dabbled in alchemy, sorcery and science. In the crypt are two of his anatomical models – strange skeletons with 'petrified' veins.

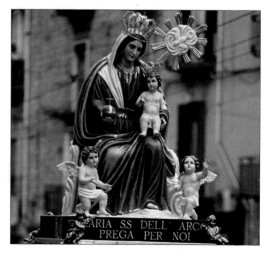

**Right:** *Most Neapolitans are religious, as demonstrated by the many processions.*

Back on Spaccanapoli, now called Via B. Croce, is the freestanding belfry of **Santa Chiara**. The entrance to the Poor Clare convent built in 1310–28 by Sancia de Mallorca, wife of King Robert the Wise is just around the corner on Via Benedetto Croce. Its erstwhile Baroque decor stripped away after bomb damage in 1943, it has several fine tombs including those of Robert the Wise (1343), by Florentine sculptors Giovanni and Pacio Bertini, and Marie de Valois. The real highlight, however, is the beautiful Gothic cloister, reached by a separate entrance on Via Santa Chiara. In 1742, Domenico Antonio Vaccaro covered the pillars and walls in a series of fabulous majolica tiles, a light-hearted decoration in contrast to the excessive church decoration of the period, but don't try to sit on the benches – the ever-officious Neapolitan guards will soon see you off. Beside the cloister is a small museum housing various church treasures.

Beyond Santa Chiara, you reach the **Piazza del Gesù Nuovo** (New Jesus Square), the main square of the old city and home to the city tourist office, with its very helpful staff.

Larger than the similar palace in Ferrara, the **Church of Gesù Nuovo** (New Church of Jesus), with its façade of diamond lozenges, was originally intended to be part

**Above:** *The magnificent Gothic cloisters of the Santa Chiara are covered in beautiful majolica tiles.*

## RENAISSANCE KING

Much that is finest and most beautiful in Naples was the inspiration of Bourbon King Charles III, son of Philip V of Spain and Elisabeth Farnese, who installed himself on the throne in 1734. Amongst his other achievements, he built the San Carlos Opera House, the Palazzo Capodimonte (to house the superb Farnese art collection that he inherited from his mother), and was responsible for starting the excavation of Pompeii.

of the Palazzo Sanseverino, but it remained unfinished and in 1584, the Jesuits converted the building into an overblown homage to Baroque indulgence, every surface patterned, decorated and/or gilded. In keeping with the theme, the 19th-century altar is inlaid with semiprecious stones. The huge marble **Guglia dell' Immacolata** (Spire of Mary Immaculata), situated in the centre of the square, was erected by the Jesuits in 1743.

Head for **Via Toledo**, busy and popular but now competing with other shopping streets in Naples. It was named after the Viceroy who demolished the city walls to build it in 1536, and leads down towards royal Naples.

### ROYAL NAPLES

Down on the seafront, near the main passenger port, the Art Deco **Stazione Marittima di Molo Beverello**, built in 1936, is at the heart of royal Naples. The formidable, crenellated **Castel Nuovo** (New Castle; Piazza Municipio), also known as Maschio Angioino (Angevin Keep) was built by the Angevins in 1279, in place of two earlier royal residences, the Castel dell'Ovo *(see* page 44) and the Castello di Capuano, now the city law courts, near the Porta di Capuana. Following a grand tradition of naming, this 'new' castle is now one of the

**Below:** *Inside the beautiful Castel Nuovo.*

oldest buildings in Naples, built originally by the Angevins in 1279. The basic shape remains that of a classic Norman castle, but the interior was heavily altered in 1443. The castle's chief asset is a magnificent 15th-century gateway, the **Arco di Trionfo di Alfonso**, designed by Francesco Laurana in 1467 to celebrate the life and achievements of the Aragonese king, Alfonso il Magnanimo (the Magnanimous). Inside, have a look at the view from the top floors, the rib-vaulted ceiling of the **Sala dei Baroni** (Barons' Hall), now the city Council Chamber, the **Museo Civico** (City Museum), and the 13th-century **Cappella Palatina** (Palatine Chapel), which tells the story of Naples through a series of 14th–19th-century paintings, sculptures and *objects d'art*.

Next to the **Castel Nuovo**, the vast dark reddish building is the **Palazzo Reale** (Royal Palace; Piazza del Plebiscito 1), built by the Spanish Viceroy in 1600, in preparation for a state visit by Philip III (which was later cancelled). Successions of Viceroys lived here in high style until 1743, when Charles III eventually moved in. Each newly arrived dynasty wished to stamp their mark on the palace and work continued up until 1843. Thirty of the State Apartments are on display, reached via an imposing double staircase. Most are richly ornamented and furnished, often in a rather cumbersome Spanish Imperial style, but two stand out above the crowd, the King's delightful little private theatre, the **Teatrino di Cort**, and the lavishly decorated 19th-century **Cappella Reale** (Royal Chapel).

The **Ala delle Feste Wing** of the palace now houses one of Italy's most important historic libraries, the **Biblioteca Nazionale** (National Library; guided visits only). Amongst its treasures are several parchments rescued from Herculaneum and some magnificently illustrated medieval manuscripts. The **Stables** are used for temporary exhibitions.

Beyond the palace stretches the huge, pedestrianized parade ground of the **Piazza del Plebiscito**, laid out by Joachim Murat in 1810 as a place for processions and festivals. On the far side, the neoclassical

## BACKGROUND READING

For some great background reading about Naples and its environs, drop in on Jeff Matthews's online *Around Naples Encyclopedia*, a true labour of love by an academic. It has hundreds of articles from the erudite to the extraordinary, plus lots of useful tourist information and links. http://faculty.ed.umuc.edu/~j matthew/naples/newAN.html

Seafront

Basilica di San Francesco di Paola is a close copy of the Pantheon in Rome, designed by Pietro Bianchi in 1817 to celebrate King Ferdinand's return to the throne.

Before leaving the piazza, stop at one of the city's oldest and most glamorous cafés, the **Caffè Gambrinus**, dating from 1860 and the literary haunt of visitors from Guy de Maupassant to Oscar Wilde. It is a charming way to while away an hour sampling delicious coffee and cake amongst the *belle époque* paintings and smart Neapolitan ladies in hats and gloves.

On one side of the next pretty little **Piazza Trieste e Trento** is the **Galleria Umberto I.** It was designed in 1887 by Emanuele Rocco as part of the Urban Renewal Plan following the cholera epidemic of 1884. The building is breathtaking, with elaborately decorated galleries, a glass and iron dome by Paolo Boubée as delicate and intricate as a spider's web and patterned marble pavements, as handsome as the similar one in Milan, but less crowded.

On the other side the **Teatro San Carlo**, Italy's oldest opera house, was first built in 1737, then rebuilt after a fire in 1816. The sumptuous interior symphony of red and gold, with 184 boxes arranged in seven tiers, is superb. Scarlatti, Bellini, Verdi and Donizetti were all amongst its Musical Directors.

## VIEW FROM BENEATH

Some 2500 years ago, the earliest inhabitants of Naples discovered that the soft tufa rock on which the city stands was easily carved into anything from wine cellars and warehouses to tunnels and catacombs. Today, this network forms almost an entirely new level to the city. Tours leave every weekend from the Caffè Gambrinus, Piazza Trieste e Trento.

## THE SEAFRONT

Around the little peninsula (or through the tunnel) from the palace is the area of **Santa Lucia**, made famous by the lyrical romantic song. Its most dramatic feature is the city's oldest castle, the strangely named **Castel dell'Ovo** (Castle of the Egg), built on a little islet, just offshore, over the remains of a Roman villa and 5th-century monastery. The first castle on the site dates to the 9th century, but it has been blown up and remodelled several times over the centuries. Its current form, from the outside, is the one given to it in 1503. It was used as a military installation until 1975, when its latest restoration turned it into a conference centre. At its foot, the **Borgo Marinaro** (fishermen's quarter) has become a trendy marina, and is filled with restaurants.

On shore, the neighbouring area is an elegant seafront promenade. It was built, along with the whole district behind it, in the 19th century, as the wealthier families moved out of the crowded city centre to what is still one of Naples' most desirable residential areas. Known as the **Lungomare**, the waterfront is a pleasant place for a stroll, but there are also one or two sights worth a visit. Not far from the

### POWER OF THE EGG

According to legend, first written down in the 14th century, the Latin poet Virgil, who was considered by many to be a sorcerer, placed a carafe containing a magic egg in the foundations of the strangely named Castel dell'Ovo (Castle of the Egg). It is said that the city will survive without any great harm as long as the egg remains intact.

**Left:** *The Castel dell'Ovo is the oldest castle in Naples, and stands over the city as if to protect it.*

**Right:** *The city's apart-ments jostle for a view of the Bay of Naples. It is no wonder why all the major powers throughout the centuries have sought to control it.*

---

## FISH DISH

Founded in 1872 by Polish naturalist Antonio Dohrn, the Naples' aquarium, the Stazione Zoologica, is the oldest in Europe. It has several rare Mediterranean species amongst the exhibits, all of which are native to the Bay of Naples. The aquarium has had mixed fortunes through the years – after the arrival of the Allies in 1943, the Neapolitans emptied the tanks and used the exhibits for a monumental celebration feast.

---

castle is the **Fontana dell'Immacolatella** (Immacolata Fountain), which was sculpted in 1601 by Michel-angelo Naccherino and Pietro Bernini. Continue from here past several of the city's finest hotels, still sumptuous with *belle époque* splendour, past the Piazza Vittoria to the sadly scruffy **Villa Comunale**, which has been a public park since 1697. It is home to the city aquarium, a number of fountains and some pleasing sculptures.

Behind it, the **Museo Villa Pignatelli** (Riviera di Chiaia) is a fascinating museum, based on the private collection of the 18th–19th century paintings, sculp-tures and ceramics of Prince Diego Aragona Pignatelle Cortes. The neoclassical villa was built in 1826 by Pietro Valente for the British Acton family, and later became the property of the Rothschilds. The stables house a collection of carriages.

At the far end, beyond another grand square, Piazza della Repubblica, **Mergellina** is the closest thing Naples has to a seaside resort, with a marina, rows of seafront cafés and restaurants , and a holiday atmosphere. On the hill above is a park which is supposed to contain the tomb of the Latin poet, Virgil. He is not there, but the Sicilian poet, Giacomo Leopardi, is.

## POSILLIPO

Beyond Mergellina, the road sweeps round up the cliff to the northern arm of the Bay of Naples and the residential suburb of **Posillipo** whose Greek name Pausilypon (meaning 'respite from anxieties') gives a remarkable clue to its role in Neapolitan life. Always a haven of tranquillity, from the 17th–19th centuries, this was the hangout of the local super-rich, who left behind some spectacular villas. Amongst the finest are Cosimo Fanzago's unfinished **Palazzo Donn'Anna** (1642), built for Donna Anna Carafa, wife of the Viceroy Filippo Ramiro Guzman; the **Villa di Sir William Hamilton**, most famous as the place where Nelson met Emma Hamilton at a dinner party thrown by her husband while the fleet was in town, the neoclassical **Villa Doria D'Angri**, the **Egyptianate Ara Votiva per I Caduti per la Patria**, begun as a mausoleum in 1883 but adopted by the city as a war memorial, and the **Villa Quercia**.

Sadly, they have been overwhelmed in recent years by high-rise development and most are virtually invisible behind high hedges and fences. However, the views from the clifftop road are incomparable and those who are prepared to walk down the steep cliff (actually the crater wall of a long dead volcano) find themselves on a charming seafront, based on the little fishing village of **Marechiaro**. The best way to see the villas is from the sea, on the Naples-Procida ferry.

## ON THE CLIFFTOP

On top of the cliff behind the town is another of the city's most desirable residential areas, **Vomero**, reached by three funicular railways. It is worth going up for the views alone, but the area also has a couple of the city's finest sights. The star-shaped **Castel Sant'Elmo** (Via Tito Angelini), which totally dominates views of the city, was built in 1537–1546 by Pedro Scriba for Viceroy Toledo to guard the outer defensive wall of the city. There is little to see inside, although it does house temporary exhibitions, but the views are superb.

Just in front of it, the **Certosa di San Martino**

### LOCK UP THE TROUBLEMAKERS

Built to defend Naples from its enemies, the Castel Sant' Elmo has never fired a shot in anger against an invader, but it did prove useful as a prison, housing amongst many others the Renaissance philosopher, Tommaso Campanella. During the Napoleon-inspired Republican Masaniello Revolt of 1799, the viceroy sheltered here from the mob. Once the rebellion was crushed, many of the ring-leaders were imprisoned behind the castle's solid walls, as were the defeated members of the 19th-century Risorgimento.

**Right:** *The suburb of Posillipo, once housing the stunning villas of the elite, but now overrun with apartment buildings.*

(Monastery of St Martin; Largo San Martino 5) has been a museum since 1866. This magnificent Carthusian monastery was originally founded by Charles of Anjou, Duke of Calabria in 1325, although the current buildings date mainly to the 16th century. The monks of San Martino lived in high style, and from the 15th–19th centuries collected around them a wonderful array of paintings, sculpture, ceramics, glass, jewellery, *presepi* and other Neapolitan crafts, most of which fetched up in the quarters of the Prior, the only member of the order technically allowed contact with the outside world. His rooms, the **Quarto del Priore** and the extravagantly Baroque church are two highlights in a fabulous museum.

Nearby, it is also worth visiting the attractive neo-classical **Villa Floridiana**, home to the **Museo Nazionale della Ceramica Duca di Martina** (Duke of Martina National Ceramic Museum; Villa Floridiana, Vomero), with an interesting collections of ceramics, majolica, glass, leather, Gothic ivory, and enamels.

Further along the ridge, towards the south of the city, is the **Palazzo Capodimonte**, the most magnificent of the royal palaces in Naples, commissioned by Charles III in 1738 partly as a hunting lodge, but mainly to house the superb Farnese art collection left to him by his mother. It was an extravagant scheme, the vast palace

## ROYAL CHINA

In the mid-18th century, with the secret of porcelain newly arrived from China, crowned heads across Europe were quick to found factories, from Limoges to Meissen. In 1743 Bourbon King Charles III set up a pavilion for the Royal Factory in the grounds of Capodimonte. It produced a distinctive 'soft paste' porcelain with elaborate frills and designs. The king loved it so much that he took his factory back to Spain with him in 1759, but the Pavilion was reopened in 1771.

surrounded by a gracious park, which included, amongst other things, a pheasantry, zoo (with lions and elephants) and a huge greenhouse for exotic fruit. In all, the project took nearly 100 years to complete. The grounds also became home to the royal porcelain works, producing some of Europe's most famous ceramics – seen in their full glory in the 3000 tiles of Capodimonte porcelain which line the palace's **Salotta di porcellana** (Porcelain Room). As the **Museo Nazionale di Capodimonte** (Capodimonte National Museum and Park; Via Miano 1), the palace now houses a superb collection of furniture, porcelain and fine art, with works by Rafael, Botticelli, Lippi, Vasari, El Greco, Caravaggio, Breughel, and Goya amongst others.

On the slopes below, just to the north of the Archaeological Museum are the old city cemeteries, with several interesting churches and intriguing, if sometimes rather grizzly, catacombs such as the huge two-storey **Catacombe di San Gennaro** (Via Capodimonte 13). Carved from the soft volcanic rock, this web of tunnels has been in use since the 2nd century, but acquired a desirable reputation when San Gennaro, patron saint of Naples, was buried here in the 6th century. All bishops of Naples were buried here until the 11th century amidst some fine 2nd–10th century frescoes and mosaics.

To the east, for a little light relief, is the **Orto Botanico** (Botanical Gardens, Via Foria 223), a lovely 12ha (30-acre) botanical garden, laid out by Joseph Bonaparte in 1807.

To the south, back at the gates of the old city, near the **Porta San Gennaro**, is the imposing **Church of San Giovanni a Carbonara** (Via San Giovanni a Carbonara 5), founded as an Augustin monastery in 1343. Highlights include its magnificent early 18th-century grand double staircase, designed by Ferdinando Sanfelice; paintings by Mattia Preti, added in 1656 as thanks for surviving the plague; the huge monumental tomb of King Ladislas (1414); the Tuscan tiled floor of the round Cappella Caracciolodel Sole (1427); and the paintings in the Cappella Caracciolo di Vico (1517).

## TOURISM OF DEATH

There are several more interesting sites near the San Gennaro Catacombs. The San Severo Catacombs (Piazza San Severo) grew up around the tomb of San Severo, Bishop of Naples (AD364–410). The Basilica di Santa Maria della Sanità (Via Sanità 124) houses the relics of a popular local saint, San Vincenzo. Under the high altar is access to more catacombs, based around the burial site of an African bishop, Settimio Celio Gaudioso who died in exile in Naples in AD452. The Cimitero delle Fontanelle (Fontanelle Cemetery; Via Fontanelle 77) is a series of large caverns hewn from the rock for mass burials of victims of the 1836 cholera epidemic.

## Naples at a Glance

### BEST TIMES TO VISIT

The ideal time is **spring** (Apr–May) and **autumn** (Sep–Oct). However, **winters** are mild and can even be sunny, and the city hotels, restaurants and sights stay open all year. **Midsummer** (Jul–Aug) can be very hot and overcrowded.

### GETTING THERE

*See* Travel Tips, page 123.

### GETTING AROUND

Naples centre is surprisingly small and you can do much of your sightseeing on foot. An excellent public transport network combines buses, metros, funiculars (up to Vomero), trams (along the shore) and suburban trains. City Sightseeing run hop-on hop-off sightseeing buses (www.city-sightseeing.com). Ask the tourist office for a transport map. Use the same tickets, called Giranapoli, on everything. Buy them in advance from stations, tobacconists or newsagents and date stamp them the first time you use them to validate them. A single allows 90 minutes of travel; a full day ticket is good value if you are travelling a lot. If you are there for over 10 days, a monthly pass is cost-effective. Don't fare dodge – there are regular inspections and stiff on-the-spot fines. A Campania Arte Card includes transport (*see* panel, page 34). Taxis are available on the street, but it is easier to call one. **Radio Taxi Partenope**, tel: 081 560 6666 or 556 0202.

### WHERE TO STAY

The best place to stay is along the Lungomare, but there are pensions and small hotels in the old town and Via Chaia area, and some grand ones on the Vomero slopes. There are cheaper hotels around the station, but walking around at night here can be dangerous.

#### LUXURY
**Consorzio Napoli Bay of Excellence**, Via Partenope 37 D, 80121 Napoli, tel: 081 764 0419, www.bayofexcellence. org A consortium of the most luxurious properties in the Bay of Naples – all on one website.
**Excelsior**, Via Partenope 48, tel: 081 764 0111, www. excelsior.it A *belle époque* seafront hotel. Spacious and elegant rooms, flawless service. Guests include royalty, artists, film stars and politicians.
**Grand Hotel Vesuvio**, Via Partenope 45, tel: 081 764 0044, www.vesuvio.it It opened on the waterfront in 1882 and retains its elegance. Caruso died here in 1921.

#### MID-RANGE
**Albergo Palazzo Decumani**, Piazza Giustino Fortunato 8, tel: 081 420 1379, www. palazzodecumani.com Chic boutique townhouse in the heart of the centro storico.
**Pinto Storey**, Via Martucci 72, tel: 081 681 260, www. pintostorey.it On the 3rd floor of a mansion block on Piazza Amedeo. Charm, antiques and a good location.

**Hotel Piazza Bellini**, Via Santa Maria di Costantinopoli 101, tel: 081 451 732, www.hotelpiazzabellini.com Stylish, funky décor in an old palazzo on the edge of the centro storico, with helpful staff and good breakfast.

#### BUDGET
**Hotel Duomo**, Via Duomo 228, tel: 081 265 988, http:// duomo.hotelsinnapoli.com Small, family-run hotel in a 19th-century building in the old town. Basic but pleasant and friendly.
**Le Stanze del Vicere**, Via Stella n. 94 (traversa Via Santa Teresa degli Scalzi), tel: 081 564 8797, www.lestanzedel vicere.it On the 2nd floor of a 17th-century palazzo near the Archaeological Museum, this is beautifully restored, and run, with a garden but no lift.
**Hotel Cimarosa**, Via Cimarosa 29, tel: 081 556 7044, www. hotelcimarosa.it Simple rooms in a Vomera apartment block, recently updated.

### WHERE TO EAT

#### LUXURY
**Da Dora**, Via F. Palasciano 28, tel: 081 680 519, www. dadora.it Delectable seafood in a charming family-run trattoria. Closed Sun; and for 15 days in Aug.
**Al Faretto**, Via Marechiaro 127, Posillipo, tel: 081 575 0407, www.alfaretto.it A little way out of the centre, but worth it for wonderful seafood on the terrace overlooking the bay.

# Naples at a Glance

**Amici Miei**, Via Monte di Dio 78, tel: 089 764 6063, www.ristoranteamicimiei.com A highly popular trattoria serving traditional Italian meats and pastas, between Chaia and the Spanish Quarter. Book ahead.

### MID-RANGE

**Ciro a Santa Brigida**, Via Santa Brigida 71, tel: 081 552 4072, www.ciroasantabrigida.com A fantastic restaurant first opened in the 1930s. Two other branches, in Mergellina and the Borgo Marinaro.

**La Barrique**, Piazzetta Ascensione 9, tel: 081 662 7218. Not cheap but a wonderful place to sample wines and grappa, while nibbling on perfectly prepared small dishes of salads and charcuterie. Weekly menu.

**Taverna dell'Arte**, Via Rampe SG Maggiore 1/A, tel: 081 552 7558, www.tavernadellarte.it Friendly; tripe and pigs' trotters on the menu. Small and popular, so book ahead.

### BUDGET

**Osteria Mattonella**, Via G. Nicotera 13, tel: 081 416 541. Family-run restaurant, with an ever changing selection of traditional food. Book ahead.

**Pizzeria Brandi**, Salita S, Anna di Palazzo 1/2 (cnr via Chiaia), tel: 081 416 928. *Margherita* pizza was invented here for Queen Margherita's 1889 visit.

**Pizzeria da Michele**, Via Cesare Sersale 1–3, tel: 081 553 9204. Best pizzas in town, but only two kinds – marinara or margherita. Closed Sun.

*Cafés*

**Gran Caffé Gambrinus**, Piazza Trieste e Trento, tel: 081 417 582. Sumptuous coffee shop, an institution since 1866.

**Pasticceria Scaturchio**, Piazza San Domenico Maggiore 19, tel: 081 551 6944. Old town patisserie. Sit in the square, watch the Sunday market and nibble a *ministeriali* (cake).

CLUBS AND BARS

**Fonoteca**, Via Morghen 31, tel: 081 556 0338, www.fonoteca.net In Vomero, lively at night with good food and music. Fronted by a CD shop, open till 01:00, very popular.

**Velvet Zone**, Via Cisterna dell' Olio 11, tel: 0339 670 0234. Videos, electronica, all-night dancing in über-cool club.

### SHOPPING

You can buy almost anything here and often for very reasonable prices – look for Italian designer clothes in the Via Chaia area. For secondhand and antiquarian books, try Via Port d'Alba, next to Piazza Dante. For food, try the delicatessens along Spaccanapoli or the back street markets in the old town. For almost anything, the main shopping street

in the city is Via Toledo.

### TOURS AND EXCURSIONS

**Consortaxi**, Piazza S. Maria La Nova 44, tel: 081 552 0205; Numero Verde: 1670 16221. Tours by taxi of Naples and the surrounding region, including Sorrento, the Amalfi Coast, Pompeii and Herculaneum.

**Chamber of Commerce Tours**. Free city and area tours every Fri night and two Sat a month. Tickets from travel agents or hotels; commentary in Italian, English, French, and German.

### USEFUL CONTACTS

*Tourist Information:*
Piazza del Gesù,
tel: 081 552 3328
or 081 551 2701,
www.regione.campania.it
*Provincial Tourist Office:*
Piazza dei Martiri 58, Cap 80121, tel: 081 410 7211. There are also kiosks at the airport and stations.

**Qui Napoli** is an essential free monthly listings magazine available from the tourist offices with detailed listings of all sights, activities and transport in the city. For more information, go to www.inaples.it

| NAPLES | J | F | M | A | M | J | J | A | S | O | N | D |
|---|---|---|---|---|---|---|---|---|---|---|---|---|
| AVERAGE TEMP. °C | 8 | 9 | 11 | 14 | 17 | 21 | 24 | 24 | 21 | 17 | 13 | 10 |
| AVERAGE TEMP. °F | 46 | 48 | 52 | 57 | 63 | 70 | 75 | 75 | 70 | 63 | 56 | 50 |
| RAINFALL mm | 116 | 85 | 73 | 62 | 44 | 31 | 19 | 32 | 64 | 107 | 147 | 135 |
| RAINFALL in | 4.6 | 3.4 | 2.9 | 2.4 | 1.7 | 1.2 | 0.8 | 1.3 | 2.5 | 4.2 | 5.8 | 5.3 |
| DAYS OF RAINFALL | 11 | 10 | 9 | 8 | 7 | 4 | 2 | 3 | 5 | 9 | 11 | 12 |

# 3
# North and West of Naples

The peninsula that reaches out into the sea and forms the beautiful northern arm of the Bay of Naples has been popular amongst both the wealthy and fishermen since the Greeks arrived in the 8th century BC. Most of its towns have now been subsumed into ribbon development, but there are still many wonderful, often sadly disregarded sights.

## THE CAMPI FLEGREI

Beyond **Posillipo**, the peninsula is known as the **Campi Flegrei** (Phlegraean or 'burning' Fields). Effectively, it sits on a giant pool of molten magma, which feeds at least 50 small volcanoes. The ancient world considered it to be a mystical location. **Lago d'Averna**, near **Pozzuoli**, is really a flooded crater, with particularly dark, lonely and atmospheric waters. Birds flying over were often asphyxiated by fumes, and thus it was regarded by both Homer and Virgil as the actual mouth of Hades (a concept that continued well into the middle ages, when Dante used it as the inspiration for his Inferno). Astonishingly, neither this nor the very real risk of eruption stopped people from settling here. At first, the Romans and Greeks set up spas, baths and temples near the hot springs, while the fertile volcanic soil encouraged the farmers and agricultural development. In recent years, it has become one of the city's most sought after commuter districts. Even more astonishingly, considering the high risks, the area is home to much of Naples's heavy industry, from steel and cement works, to chemical plants.

### DON'T MISS

**★★★ Caserta:** home to one of Europe's largest and most ostentatious, if not most beautiful palaces.
**★★★ Montecassino:** a grand Benedictine monastery, lavishly endowed with beautiful art.
**★★ Pozzuoli:** the bubbling steaming Solfatara.
**★★ Avellino, Aversa and other small towns:** dot the routes north of Naples, and you should not miss a visit to antique **Capua** with its unusual town plan.

**Opposite:** *The gardens at Caserta are well worth a visit.*

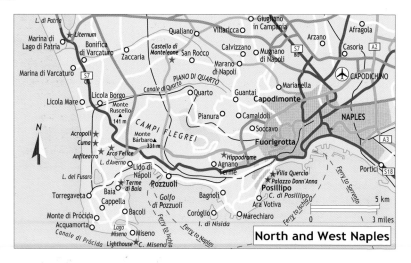

**North and West Naples**

## POZZUOLI

Although probably first inhabited in the 7th century BC, it was in 530BC that some Samian exiles founded the first official town of **Dikaiarchia**. The town flourished, becoming an important trade and industrial centre under the Romans, who arrived in 194BC and changed its name to **Puteoli**. Amongst its more lucrative contracts was landing all the wheat consumed by Rome, imported from the Eastern Empire. By the 5th century AD, the barbarians arrived and its fortunes declined. The level of the land dropped by 12m (39ft) between the 2nd century BC and the 11th century AD, and the harbour silted up, then drowned. The land only began to rise again in the 17th century.

Today, the reason most people visit Pozzuoli is to see the extraordinary **Solfatara** (Via Solfatara 161), a shallow volcanic crater about 2km (1.5 miles) in diameter. Although it was formed about 4000 years ago and last erupted in AD1198, it still provides the most visible volcanic activity in the region. It has an entertaining collection of fumaroles (jets of steam and carbon dioxide), solfataras (jets of water vapour and sulphuric acid), bubbling sand, burping pools of boiling mud and colourful sulphur-yellow or reddish-purple stained rocks.

### TIDAL TOWN

The **height** of the land around the **Campi Flegrei** has **fluctuated** over the centuries by several metres, according to the level of the giant magma pool on which the area rests. Since the 1960s, the level of this **seismic activity** (known as bradyseism) has been increasing steadily and so full that the town of **Pozzuoli** has physically **risen** by nearly 8m (26ft). Over the past five years there has been increasing activity too.

Relatively few of the ancient city's civic buildings have survived. The exception is the remarkably preserved **amphitheatre** (Via Terracciano), built in AD69–79. Seating 40,000 people, it had a sophisticated system of underground storage and mechanical trapdoors and elevators, used when staging wild animal spectaculars. Near the harbour, another fine Roman building was long thought to be the Temple of Serapide, but is now known to have been the rather more prosaic **Macellum** or city market (Piazza Serapide).

Unfortunately, due to the seismic upheavals, the pretty **Rione Terra** (old town) near the harbour had to be evacuated in 1970. Restoration work is now underway, but until the district and its buildings have been properly stabilized, they remain off limits.

The **Citta della Scienza** (via Coroglio 104, Bagnoli, tel: 081 242 0024, www.cittadellascienza.it), between Posillipo and Pozzuoli, is a Neapolitan science museum in an old chemical factory – slightly po-faced but with some interesting exhibits and a good alternative to statuary if you have restive children with you.

**TOP TIP**

Although the **Cumana train** stops in **Pozzuoli**, it is better to take a **bus** from the **Lungomare** in Naples to the entrance of the **Solfatara**, then go on to visit the town. This means that you can do the steep walk downhill and take the train back into Naples from the town centre.

**Below:** *The 1st-century Flavian amphitheatre in Pozzuoli was very impressive, seating up to 40,000 spectators.*

### CONSULTING THE
### ORACLE

As in Delphi, consulting
the Oracle at Cumae was
a serious business. People
travelled hundreds of miles
to discover their fate or seek
wisdom over troubling ques-
tions. There were always too
many seekers for the Oracle
to handle and many had to
wait days or weeks, in prayer
or fasting, before their number came up. Before entering
they prayed, scrubbed clean,
and offered sacrifices. Once
they returned from the cave,
in a trance-like state, priests
were on hand to transcribe
and interpret their experi-
ences for them.

# CUMA

As the road heads west across the neck of the peninsula, along the old Roman Via Domitiana, it passes a
grand triumphal arch, the **Arco Felice**, and Lago
d'Averno. Cuma is believed to be one of the oldest
settlements in southern Italy. Until about the 3rd century BC, it reigned supreme but declined rapidly as
Puteoli (Pozzuoli) flourished. Relatively small areas
have yet to be fully excavated, but the **Parco Archeologico** (Via Acropoli) is still impressive, with temples to
Jupiter and Apollo. Its most renowned attraction was
the Oracle. The **Antro della Sibilla** (Sibyl's Grotto) is a
cave carved from the soft tufa, which was supposedly
home to virgin priestesses of the Cult of Apollo, who
were visited by many travellers, even Aeneas according
to the *Aeneid*. Possibly these excavations might have
been military tunnels or a Greek tomb.

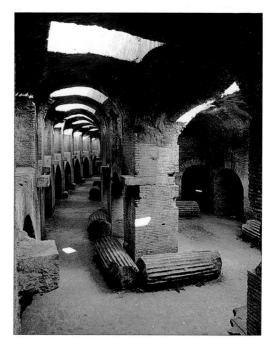

**Right:** *The Flavian
amphitheatre contained a
network of underground
cells. Wild animals were
kept in these cells, and
used to fight as part of
the entertainment.*

## BAIA

Along the peninsula are interesting sites: the Roman fleet was based at **Miseno**, but little remains. Their greatest legacy is their massive underground water storage cistern, the **Piscina Mirabile** (Via A. Greco), carved from the tufa at **Bacoli**. Measuring 70m x 25.5m x15m, with a vaulted ceiling resting on 48 giant pillars, it is the largest known Roman reservoir in the world.

**Baia** was a popular Roman spa. What is left stands high over the sea: there are fine views. It was favoured by Caligula, Claudius, Nero and Domitian, but much is now under water. The finest of the many remains include the **Terme Romana** (Roman Baths, Via Fusaro 35) and the **Museo Archeologico dei Campi Flegrei** (Phlegraean Fields Archaeology Museum). Rooms in this towering castle are filled with finds from the locality including notable heads and elegant sculptures. Unusual Roman figures have had heads ruined by marine life for they protruded above protective sand. **Castello Aragonese** was built by a Spanish viceroy in 1538.

## CAPUA

This warmly enclosing city, with its squares, pillars and arcades beyond a river promenade, was a prime source for Shakespeare's plots: ancient stories abound in Capua. It was here that Hannibal dallied in a luxurious life, while its gateway marked the edge of the Holy Roman Empire. The Roman town lies beyond the borders of the 'modern' Capua, constructed in a tight net of narrow arched streets within an unusual triangular plan. Many of its buildings are made of Roman stone. The cathedral is a compilation of periods, much rebuilt since construction 11 centuries ago. Even then, bits were recycled – some of its Corinthian columns belong to 3rd century Rome, rather than the Romanesque. Around the cathedral, narrow alleys and churches are packed into the confines of the old ramparts. Don't miss the **Piazza Giudici** with a Baroque church, and the town hall.

### CAPUA

Capua may be redolent of Rome but it has much more history to offer. The site itself is an ancient one, and has been lived on for thousands of years, as revealed by a fascinating and varied collection of earth goddesses of the 7th to the 1st century BC. These can be seen at the Museo Campano, by the Via Duomo. There are also fine sculptures from the date of 1239, marking the boundary of an emperor's lands.

The **Museo Campano**, an excellent small museum located at the corner of the Via Duomo, houses a collection of both local Roman and medieval sculpture, mosaics too. The large collection of images of earth goddesses, some over 2500 years old, is an indication of Capua's long history.

### CASERTA

In 1750, Bourbon King Charles III, looked enviously on Versailles and began to spend. Choosing a site safely inland, he commissioned locally born painter, Luigi Vanvitelli, to create for him the palace to put all others in the shade. Construction went ahead at full speed for over 20 years, before limping on into the following century. What Vanvitelli created is extraordinary more for its size than its beauty. The Royal Palace (measuring a staggering 247m x 184m) has 34 staircases linking 1200 rooms,

**Below:** *The magnificent Caserta Palace.*

arranged around four identical courtyards. It is nearly double the size of Versailles, although only half that of the Bourbons' other monstrosity, the Escorial, near Madrid. Unusually, the public façade is far less decorative than the back elevation, designed to be seen only by the court. Only the royal apartments and the gardens are open to the public, but still allow a full day's touring.

The many carvings, sculptures, paintings, panels, gilded furnishing and elaborate marble halls are all designed to impress and they cannot fail to do so – although sadly, more for their opulence than their artistic merit. The highlights undoubtedly are the magnificent grounds, with formal vistas and walkways, fountains and lakes, and a luxuriantly planted English garden. For those with weary feet, there is a bus which runs around the grounds to various key points.

During World War II, the palace was used as the **Allied Military Headquarters** and it was here that Germany officially surrendered in 1945.

The town that grew up around the palace is uninspiring, but 10km (6 miles) away, on the slopes of Mount Virgo is **Caserta Vecchia**. This charming, sleepy old place was probably founded by the Lombards in the 8th century. Because it has virtually been ignored since the 18th century, its medieval centre, clustered around a beautiful 12th-century cathedral, has survived almost intact.

## NORTH TO SESSA AURUNCA

In the extreme west of Campania, below the hills and above Capua and Caserta, this stretch of coast running as far as the border with Lazio, is often overlooked. You can drive along a shore road, the S7, or ascend inland through fine scenery as far as **Sessa Aurunca**, which is a town of Roman origins with important remains of the period – notably a theatre and a bathhouse as well as a fine Roman bridge outside the little town. It is a particularly colourful place with its green and yellow roof tiles and its 12th-century cathedral decorated with fine bas reliefs. There is a ruined castle too, beyond the

### GLORIOUS GARDENS

Caserta's gardens remind you of another time – a melancholic lost world which was a backdrop for 18th-century Neapolitan fops and their ladies. This ghostly French garden with its monumental sculpture rising along parterres and above pools, specimen trees, fountains that once played to the Bourbon court, sombre allées and vistas, is perhaps the most touching image that people take away from this rather heavy and ponderous palace of pleasure.

**MONTECASSINO**

It is hard to believe the building was ruined by bombardments in World War II. It has actually been destroyed four times since being established as the mother-house of the Benedictine order in AD 529. The hard-fought offensive of 1943–44 lasted eight months after the Allies had liberated Naples. It is much visited by old soldiers, American, British, Polish and French; the last two armies suffered particularly. The Nazi forces quitted the abbey on 17 May 1945, leaving open the road to Rome.

centre, sternly medieval with a square tower. Nearby is a large beach called **Baia Domizia**.

Go down 6km (4 miles) to the small town of **Carinola**. The medieval town also has a castle whose notable 15th-century duomo owes much of its design to the vast hilltop abbey of Montecassino, in nearby Lazio. The mother-house of the Benedictine order, containing the tomb of St Benedict, Montecassino dominates the surrounding area. An amazing aspect is the steep road climbing the hill. Once at the abbey be prepared for the most sumptuous interiors with much use of marble, stucco and gilding in the reconstructed church. In the **museum** are works of art that escaped the heavy bombardment to which the abbey was subject in 1944 before being captured by the Allies.

Other interesting towns up from the coast are **Teano**, with a Roman ampitheatre which dates from just after Hannibal sacked the town around the 4th century BC. **Calvi** has a near-complete Roman town laid out beside its cathedral. If you want to get to **Roccamonfina** at the base of Monte Ste Croce, walk through deep chestnut woods to see a notable cloister at the Monastery Santa Maria. Water buffalo in flat fields provide mozzarella cheese offered for sale along coastal roads.

**Right:** *Waterfalls and fountains in the Caserta gardens.*

# North and West of Naples at a Glance

Spring and autumn are ideal, warm and sunny. Midsummer can be too hot and crowded for heavy-duty sightseeing. Mild in winter – this really is a year-round destination.

Two privately operated railway lines, the Circumflegrea (www.sepsa.it), from and Ferrovia Cumana along the northern arm of the Bay, link Naples with towns to the west, including Pozzuoli and Cumae. Both depart from Montesanto Station (tel: 081 551 3328) every 10–20mins. For Solfatara, it is best to take the bus from the Lungomare in Naples to the entrance of the Solfatara, when finished there continue down to Pozzuoli railway station. It will save you a long, steep walk up hill. Giranapoli tickets accepted on bus and trains. The easiest way to get to Caserta, 27km (17 miles) from Naples, is by train from the Central Station. From Caserta, there are regular buses to Capua, but you will need a car or taxi to visit Caserta Vecchia.

*LUXURY*
**The Grand Hotel Vanvitelli**, Viale Carlo III, 81020 S, San Marco Evangelista (Ce), tel: 0823 217 111, fax: 0823 421 330, www.grandhotelvanvitelli.it Top-class business hotel, luxurious rooms, near the Reggia. Pool, garage and parking lot.

**Jolly Hotel Caserta**, Via V Veneto 9, Caserta 81100, tel: 0823 325 222, www.jollyhotelcaserta.it A comfortable chain hotel with full facilities, close to the Reggia.

*MID-RANGE*
**Villa de Pertis Hotel**, Via Ponti 30, S. Giorgio 81010, Dragoni, tel/fax: 0823 866 619, www.villadepertis.it Restored country house hotel about 25km (16 miles) from Caserta, with panoramic views of the Matese Mountains. Terraced restaurant, good food.

*BUDGET*
**Volcana Solfatara**, Via Solfatara 16, Pozzuoli, tel: 081 526 7413, www.solfatara.it/camping This is the nearest camp site to the centre of Naples.

*LUXURY*
**Vairo del Volturno**, Via IV Novembre 60, Vairano Patenora, Caserta, tel: 0823 643 018, www.vairodelvolturno.com Chef Renato Martino is proudly sporting his first Michelin star for an imaginative mix of local tradition and modern flair, with several tasting menus on offer.

**Osteria dei Nobiluomini**, Piazza de Renzis 6, Capua, tel: 0823 620 062, www.osteriadeinobiluomini.it A neat restaurant, five years old, with good, reasonably priced local dishes.

*MID-RANGE*
**Antica Locanda**, Piazza della Seta, Caserta, tel: 0823 305 444. Recommended trattoria in Caserta, serving a mix of pasta and seafood. Excellent. Closed Sun lunch and Mon, and from 8–22 Aug.

**Agriturismo Il Casolare di Tobia**, Asolare, Via Selvatico, Contrada Coste dei Fondi di Báia, Báia 80070, tel: 081 523 5193, www.datobia.it A delightful small restaurant with four charmingly decorated bedrooms inside a now extinct volcanic crater near Baia, between Pozzuoli and Cumae. The food is traditional Neapolitan. No credit cards. Book ahead. No dinner on Sun. Closed Mon.

**Alla Tana del Lupo**, Via Lupara 1, Casertavecchia, tel: 0823 371 333, www.allatanadellupo.it Great food including wood-fired pizzas served in imaginative settings, with a flamboyant owner.

**Trattoria di Mare Mobydick**, Via dell'Emporio 17, Zona Porto, Pozzuoli, tel: 081 526 7934. In spite of the slightly off-putting name, this is a great seaside trattoria, with a fine line in seafood pastas.

*Tourist Information*
*Caserta*
c/o Palazzo Reale, tel: 0823 321 137, www.eptcaserta.it
*Pozzuoli*
Via Campi Flegrei 3, tel: 081 526 639, www.infocampiflegrei.it

# 4
# Under the Volcano

South of the city, the **Bay of Naples** stretches out in a long curve, its flat farmlands totally dominated by the giant, rust-red cone of Mount Vesuvius, the most active volcano on mainland Europe and probably the world's most famous. It has rumbled a lot over the millennia but its infamy really stems from one particularly vicious eruption in AD79 when it deeply buried the thriving Roman towns of Pompeii and Herculaneum, preserving them for posterity in ash and mud. Today, Pompeii is, without doubt, the most complete and exciting ancient city in the world, and while much of Herculaneum remains buried under modern Ercolano, now a suburb of expanding Naples, the relatively small area of excavations open to the public is a compelling glimpse of everyday life, Roman style. Allow at least two days to explore the area.

## VESUVIO (VESUVIUS)

Although the whole Bay of Naples rests on a sea of molten lava, from the Campi Flegrei to the north west of Naples to the thermal springs of Ischia, Mount Vesuvius is the undoubted king, a towering cone that has spewed romance and tragedy into the local air again and again through the centuries. The volcano's spirit is a lively one and locals are never sure when the mountain will perform again. The last seismic activity in the area was a relatively mild earthquake in 1980, but there hasn't been an eruption since 1944. There was severe damage to property, but the slow-moving lava field allowed all but 27 people, killed by falling masonry, to reach safety.

### DON'T MISS

**★★★ Pompeii**: Rome's finest legacy, trapped in time under volcanic mud and ash.
**★★★ Mt Vesuvius**: The volcano responsible for destroying Pompeii and Herculaneum, mainland Europe's most active volcano.
**★★★ Ercolano**: (Herculaneum) This was a thriving town with a seafront. It is still being excavated, so one can expect more discoveries.

**Opposite:** *A statue found at Ercolano (Herculaneum). The town was destroyed in 79AD, during the eruption of Vesuvius.*

**Right:** *The ancient site of Herculaneum is situated below the modern town. Even though the area is still being excavated, it gives a good impression of the town plan.*

Mount Vesuvius (1281m/4203ft) first blew itself into existence about 12,000 years ago. Since then it has erupted regularly, with over 100 recorded eruptions since AD79, although only those in 1631, 1794 and 1944 have caused really severe damage. Today, only a wisp of smoke deep inside the high crater shows a glimmer of life, but vulcanologists are far from sanguine. About 8km (5 miles) below the surface, the magma chamber is as active as ever, with molten lava climbing slowly up the pipe. There is little sign of it because the last eruption plugged the top of the pipe and geologists fear that next time the mountain blows, it will do so with the explosive force of a giant pressure cooker, literally lifting the top off the mountain.

It was this type of explosion which caused such devastation on the 24th August, AD79, when a mushroom cloud shot over 30km (19 miles) into the air, and several metres of asphyxiating ash and pumice rained down on Pompeii. A couple of days later, as the wind died, the cloud collapsed and a tidal wave of super-heated rock, ash and dust, reaching temperatures of over 475°C (887°F), swept down the slopes at 160kph (100mph). It was this pyroclastic flow that

## A TOUGH HIKE

There used to be a chair lift to the top of Mount Vesuvius, but since it collapsed, ecologists seem bizarrely to feel that the tramp of hundreds of weary feet is better for the environment. Now the only way to get to the top (1281m/ 4163ft) is on foot. The path is only about 600m (650 yd) long, but it winds steeply up the slope and takes most people 30–45 minutes. Avoid the midday heat as there is no shade. Wear sensible walking shoes, a hat and take some water.

finally buried the stunned cities, killing thousands as it passed. The horror was unimaginable then – but this time there are potentially nearly 2 million people living in the path of destruction, and the only evacuation plan is ill-conceived and unworkable, based on two weeks' notice of an eruption. Anything better will take some 10 years to put into place.

Yet nothing seems to deter locals and visitors alike. More and more houses are built on the slopes, while hundreds flock up the mountain each day to see the magnificent views and stare awe-struck into the depths of the huge crater, 200m (656ft) deep and 600m (1969ft) in diameter. Those with the time can walk right around the rim, but it is no longer possible to climb down inside.

On the way down, try and stop at the **Osservatorio Vesuviana** (Vesuvius Observatory), where there is a fascinatingly multicoloured collection of volcanic rocks on display. It was built as a research centre by Ferdinand II in 1841–45 and is still in use today.

### Herculaneum

## ERCOLANO (HERCULANEUM)

From Ercolano station, walk down the hill about 300m
(329yd) to the gate of Herculaneum, said by ancient
historian Dionysius of Halicarnassos to have been
founded by Heracles (Hercules) himself. The view from
above gives a remarkable insight into the town plan, even
though a relatively small area has been excavated –
modern Ercolano is built on top of much of the ancient
city. Herculaneum is far smaller than Pompeii, but in many
ways it is just as atmospheric and more friendly on the
feet – you can explore it easily within a couple of hours.

The town's early history is unclear, but it was
probably founded in the 7th century BC. Until AD 79,
Herculaneum and Pompeii both stood on the seashore –
the eruption dropped so much mud and rock into the
water that it pushed the shoreline out by 2km (1.2 miles).
The Romans arrived in about 290BC, and the town
became a thriving holiday resort, with a population of
about 5000. It was of less importance than Pompeii, but
popular amongst patrician families who knocked down
the seaward wall to give their villas uninterrupted views.

Herculaneum was never buried under the initial car-
pet of ash that fell on Pompeii. For years archaeologists
believed that the people had managed to escape the
catastrophe of the eruption as only six bodies were
found in the streets. In the 1980s, new excavations
uncovered the ghastly truth. As the boiling mud cas-
caded through the streets, the residents fled towards the
water where they were trapped, taking refuge in the
seafront warehouses below the patrician villas, now
grimly full of hundreds of badly burned skeletons.

The lava flow proved far more kind to posterity and
many of the houses and shops here have survived
remarkably intact, with second storeys, wooden
balconies, doors, staircases and wall paintings still
in situ. In one house, 18th-century archaeologists discovered a library of 2000 papyrus scrolls. If you lift up
your eyes, the ancient streets merge remarkably with
those of the modern town. Surprisingly little has
changed here in the last 2000 years.

Take time to wander the streets, peering into houses so vividly alive it seems as if the residents have just popped out for a minute. Some are highly decorative, such as the wealthy **Casa dell'Albergo**, the **Casa di Nettuno e Anfitrite** (House of the Neptune and Amphritite Mosaic), whose summer dining room is lavishly ornamented by mosaic, the obviously named **Casa del Atrio o Mosaico** (House of the Mosaic Atrium), and the **Casa del Rilievo di Telefo** (House of the Relief of Telephus), with magnificent marble decoration, including a bas-relief of the myth of Telephus. Many of the frescoes show signs of restoration, following an earthquake in AD63 which caused a great deal of structural damage. Many fine sculptures, including two elegant statues of stags found in the **Casa dei Cervi** (House of the Stags) are now in the Naples museum.

The forum and main public buildings have never been found, although archaeologists have a good idea of where they are. The public face of the city is most evident in the two **Terme** (Baths), remarkably similar to a modern Turkish Bath, with separate sections for men and women, hot, tepid and cold pools and a central courtyard for social lounging. Several apartment blocks and shops, such as the **Casa a Graticcio** and three-storey **Casa del Tramezzo di Legno**, are instantly recognizable while the large **palaestra** (gymnasium), to the far side of the site, has a temple, pools, training grounds and offices. The theatre is visitable, just to the left of the main site, off the road to Naples.

### ROYAL FASCINATION

Charles, the Bourbon king of Naples, who was a great devotee of history, funded the first proper archaeological studies of Pompeii in 1738. Fascinated by the volcano and the excavations, he chose to build his new palace at nearby Porticci, creating at the same time the Palazzo Caramanico as an archaeological museum. In his footsteps trailed the nobility who built a series of magnificent, if now sadly crumbling, 18th- and 19th-century villas. These villas stretch along what is now known as the Miglio d'Oro (Golden Mile).

**Right:** *The Via dei Sepolcri in ancient Pompeii.*
**Opposite:** *Pompeii's amphitheatre was used for gladiatorial battles.*

---

### FIT FOR AN EMPRESS

Although it is not definite that Villa Oplontis belonged to Nero's second wife, Poppea Sabina, its vast size and lavish decoration as well as inscriptions found here make it seem likely. Originally the unstable emperor's mistress, he repudiated his first wife and sent Poppea's first husband out of town to clear the way for the marriage. It was not her best move. She died in AD65 when Nero kicked her in the womb in a fit of rage.

---

### TO THE MANOR BORN

Suburban villas such as Villa Oplontis are probably the equivalent of the modern European stately home or manor house, with a finely designed dwelling set around the courtyard at the centre of extensive gardens. This would be used by the owners – who almost certainly also had at least one town house. The next section, still comfortable, but less fashionably decorated would be the home of the farmer and his family. The third would house the various barns, outhouses and offices. The whole complex would be surrounded by farmlands.

---

## SOUTH ALONG THE COAST

The coast road, the S18, south of Ercolano winds round the foot of the mountain through several interesting towns. The first stretch passes the run-down 18th-century villas of the **Miglio d'Oro** (Golden Mile) on its way into Portici, whose 17th-century incarnation featured in Auber's opera *Muette di Portici*. In the 18th century, King Charles built a new palace, the Reggia, here, close to his beloved excavations. In 1839, Italy's first railway line was completed, linking the royal palaces in Naples and Portici.

The **Reggia** (Via Università 100, Portici, tel: 081 775 4850) escaped the terminal decay of most of the surrounding villas by housing the local Department of Agriculture. It was recently restored to full glory and is open by appointment or for special exhibitions. It is, however, possible to visit **Villa Campolieto**, **Villa Ruggiero**, and **Villa Favorita Marine Park** (mornings only, closed Mon; the gardens are free, entry fee for the villas and audio guide). Start at Villa Campolieto (Corso Resina 283, Ercolano, tel: 081 732 2134) and either walk or get parking instructions.

A little further south, **Torre de Greco**, named after the surrounding 'Greek' vineyards, also lay in the path of several eruptions – it has several times been laid to waste by the volcano but always rises again. Interestingly its many souvenir shops make use of volcanic stone as well as coral to make brooches and beads.

**Torre Annunziata** has also has also been in the direct line of the fire, often destroyed yet just as constantly revived. Here factories turn out streams of pasta. It is more notable (certainly more interesting) for being the location of an ancient Roman palace, the **Villa Oplontis** (Via Sepolcri 1), which is open to the public and well worth a stop. A large, well excavated structure, it shows the sites of the slave quarters and also that of the Empress – it reputedly belonged to Poppaea, wife of Nero. The villa is noted for its carefully conserved wall paintings, landscapes, portraits, flowers and fountains with the peacock a frequent image.

## POMPEII

First founded in the 8th century BC by Greek settlers, the town, now far inland and dry, stood on the marshy curve of an oxbow lake at the mouth of the Sarno River. From the 6th century BC, it seems likely that there were Etruscan settlers in the area and from the 5th century BC, it was invaded by the Samnites, later coming under Roman supervision. It remained faithful to Rome during the Social War of 89BC, but followed the wrong man in an internal squabble soon afterwards and was conquered by the dictator Sulla after that. He placed his nephew in charge, renamed Colonia Veneria Cornelia Pompeii, after its conqueror, Pompey, and his favourite

### STURDY SHOES REQUIRED

Pompeii may not have been huge, but when you have a whole town to explore, it takes time. Go early and allow a whole day, take a hat, water, comfortable shoes, a good map and guidebook (audio-guide available at the site). Don't believe those who say you can't enter a building except on a guided tour – just follow the group in front. If you do choose to do a tour, most last about two hours and follow one of three set routes around selected highlights.

goddess, Venus, to whom he built a magnificent temple on the forum. Over the next few years, 2000 favoured legionaries were granted lands and property in and around the town. Gradually Roman and Samnite cultures merged. There is still clear evidence of both.

By the 1st century AD, Pompeii was a thriving market town with a population of about 10,000 (of whom about 60 per cent were freemen, the rest slaves), serving the local agricultural community and trading far afield. Surrounded by a 3km (2-mile) defensive wall, with eight city gates, the city is laid out on a classic grid of narrow paved streets surrounding a central forum. It had an excellent social life, with numerous inns and hotels, an amphitheatre (for spectaculars), theatre, smaller odeon, two gymnasia and a large forum surrounded by temples and imposing administrative buildings. It was also politically active, with election 'posters' found grafittied onto the walls. In AD62, the area was rocked by a massive earthquake and buildings were still being restored or replaced when the volcano erupted in AD79.

## Destruction and Rediscovery

At first, as the mountain blew its top, a rain of ash fell upon the town burying it several metres deep, but it was not this which caused the final devastation. As archaeologists dug through the layers, they found evidence

**Pompeii**

0 — 400 m
0 — 400 yd

Villa dei Misteri
Villa di Diomede
Villa di Cicerone
Casa del Chirurgo
Porta di Vesuvio
Porta di Capua
Porta di Sarno
Porta Ercolano
Porta Marina
Porta di Nocera
Porta di Stabia
Torre X
Torre di Mercurio XI
Torre XII
House of Marcus Lucretius Fronto
House of the Silver Wedding
House of Obelius Firmus
House of the Centennial
Central Baths
House of Orpheus
House of Venus
House of Loreius Tibertinus
House of the Orchard
House of the Cryptoporticus
House of Cornelius Rufus
Garden of the Fugitives
Brothel
Amphitheatre
Palestra Grande
Necropolis of Porta Nocera
Administrative Offices
Railway Station
Entrance
Auditorium
Via dei Sepolcri
Via delle Tombe
Viale dei Misteri
Via di Mercurio
Vicolo di Mercurio
Via della Fortuna
Via di Nola
Via dell'Abbondanza
Via Stabiana
Via di Nocera
Via Plinio
Viale Al Teatri
NAPLES
SALERNO

1. Basilica
2. Temple of Apollo
3. Forum
4. Antiquarium
5. Temple of Venus
6. Temple of Vespasian
7. Temple of Jupiter
8. Assembly Room
9. Building of Eumachia
10. House of the Vettii
11. House of the Faun
12. House of the Large Fountain
13. House of the Golden Cupids
14. House of the Tragic Poet
15. Forum Baths
16. Stabian Baths
17. House of the Menander
18. Triangular Forum
19. Large Theatre
20. Small Theatre
21. Arcaded Court of the Gladiators
22. House of Sallust

that people had managed to crawl out of hiding holes and up on top of the ash, bringing with them treasured possessions. In the calm before the ultimate storm, the citizens must have felt that however desperate the damage, they still had a chance to rebuild their lives. Then, as in Herculaneum, the pyroclastic flow struck the town, a flood of molten mud, rock and lava which hit without warning, searing the flesh from the terrified inhabitants as it swept across the town, and down to the sea. Some undoubtedly escaped, but evidence of more than 5000 bodies has been found to date.

The area remained inhabited, but the town was never rebuilt and over the centuries, it was completely forgotten. In the late 16th century, architect, Domenico Fontana, discovered a few inscriptions while building a tunnel, but nothing much more happened until 1748 when Bourbon King Charles III took personal charge. Since then, archaeologists have worked on the site, virtually without interruption. The whole town has been identified and around 80 per cent of it has been uncovered and restored. Most of the more fragile finds

## THE LITTLE DETAILS

It is surprising to see what survived and what was preserved by the great eruption of Vesuvius in AD79. At Pompeii daily life is revealed, often touchingly, in stone streets rutted with cart tracks, gardens, fast food stalls, a beware of the dog sign, an unfinished plate of pasta and beans (still a local speciality), or the illicit presence of an elegant woman in the barracks of the gladiators that fatal afternoon.

**Opposite:** *The streets of Pompeii are lined with ancient buildings.*

## PLASTER CAST

In 1860, archaeologist Giuseppi Fiorelli began finding strangely shaped holes in the solidified ash of Pompeii. Curiosity to the fore, he poured in some liquid plaster to see what was inside. What he found was the horrifying form of a human writhing in death throes. Many more of these people have since been found, providing Pompeii's most memorable images.

are now in the Archaeological Museum in Naples, but there is still the most extraordinarily complete record of life – literally frozen on a single day. Even the thousands of tourists who flock here each year simply repeople the streets and add a realistic bustle to the proceedings.

### Highlights

The main entrance to the site is through the ancient **Porta Marina** (Sea Gate) from where a main road leads straight up, past the **Basilica**, home of the law courts and administrative offices, and 3rd century BC **Temple of Apollo** to the **Forum**. This huge arcaded area (32m x 142m) was the central focus of the city, a combination of market, social hangout and official meeting place. Surrounding it are various important public buildings, including the **Antiquarium**. Rebuilt in 1948, it now houses a number of small finds, including the famous plaster casts of people and animals, the last few remnants of Sulla's famous **Temple of Venus**, along with **Temples to Vespasian and Jupiter**, three administrative offices, the **Assembly Room**, the **Building of Eumachia**, the home of the corporation of fullers and dyers used for public auctions, and the covered market.

**Right:** *The Forum served as the commercial, religious and political centre of this Roman resort.*

Before heading further into town, turn left along the line of the walls and head out of the Porto Ercolano, down the statue-lined **Via dei Sepolcri**, through the city's most affluent and beautiful cemetery to the magnificently decorated **Villa dei Misteri** (House of Mysteries). Originally built around the 2nd century BC, this was heavily restored in approximately 60BC and again just before the eruption. With the main rooms beautifully lined with figurative and *trompe l'oeil* frescoes, and a series of small courtyards and terraces that point to gracious living, this was also very much a working farm with wine presses and servants' quarters.

Thread your way back towards the forum through the narrow streets of Pompeii's wealthiest quarter, where the Vicolo di Mercurio, Via delle Terme and Via della Fortuna are home to several fine patrician villas. Those particularly worth a visit include the **House of the Vettii** (recently restored), whose most famous decorations include a rather startling depiction of the well-endowed Priapus; the palatial **House of the Faun**, the largest house in Pompeii, covering nearly 3000m² (9843 sq ft), and home to one of the world's finest known mosaics – a huge tableau of Alexander the Great defeating the Persians at the battle of Issos; the **House of the Large Fountain**, the **House of the Golden Cupids**, and the **House of the Tragic Poet**, most famous for its mosaic 'Beware of the Dog' sign, now in the Naples museum. Just before you reach the Forum, on Via del Foro, you pass the modern restaurant/coffee shop and the ancient **Forum Baths**, a large, elaborate complex built soon after the Roman conquest, with fine stucco ornamentation, frescoes and mosaic floors.

From the forum, turn into **Via dell'Abbondanza** – Main Street, Pompeii. Quite extraordinarily complete, with many of its buildings still reaching double storeys, this leads right across the city past a whole series of highly decorated villas, interspersed with shops. A short way down on the left-hand side, the Vicolo del

## CORALS AND CAMEOS

At Pompeii there are several good outlets for cameos and corals, which are regenerating along the coast. Although the stalls abound with the stuff, it's wise to use one of the established permanent shops where you get guarantees of good work. You see shell cameos being made, and you can also use credit cards.

## FAST-FOOD STALLS

On many of the street corners you will see counter tops with holes in them. These belonged to the city's *thermopilia*, or fast-food stalls. Tiny, one-room outlets, open to the street, some had a few chairs, but most only had a counter with holes set in it for jars of food and drink, an oven behind to heat the food and water for hot wine in winter. Then, as now, the local café/bar was an integral part of Italian life.

**Right:** *Appropriately named for a Roman theatre, Teatro Grande was a place to see the classic masked dramas and comedies citizens loved.*

Lupanare leads to the graphically decorated **Brothel**. Back on the main road, a short distance further on, you come to the **Stabian Baths**, one of the oldest buildings in the city, originally built in the 3rd–4th century BC, but later expanded, renovated and redecorated, with a series of elaborate bathrooms surrounding a huge open courtyard or palaestra, used for physical exercise.

At the far end of Via dell'Abbondanza lies the huge oval **Amphitheatre**, the oldest known in the world, dating to 80–70BC, with space for about 20,000 spectators. Next to it, the **Palaestra Grande** (Large Palaestra or sports field) with a pool and fields was built for military training and youthful gymnastics during the reign of Augustus. From here, Via di Nocera leads down to a city gate, while off to the right, circling the current excavations, you head for the **Garden of the Fugitives**, a former vineyard in which 27 contorted plaster bodies lie where the fleeing people fell.

Head back towards the main road, and walk back to the centre along the road parallel to Via dell' Abbondanza, passing two more particularly fine villas, the **House of the Menander**, and the **House of the Ceii**, with electioneering slogans still visible on the wall. Beyond these, Via Stabia leads down to the **Triangular Forum**, a small piazza at the centre of the entertainment quarter, surrounded by the **Theatre** (still used in summer), **Odeon** (originally used for concerts), and **Arcaded Court of the Gladiators**.

## FIVE-STAR HOTEL

Classical remains are still being uncovered, and parts of Pompeii remain unexplored. The most recent discovery, announced in early 2000, was of an inn outside Pompeii. But what an inn! Buried under 4m (13ft) of solidified ash in the great eruption, and later flooded, this was described as being an hotel of great luxury, an establishment for wealthy visitors to the city. It contains five large reception rooms complete with dining couches, fountains, wide windows and wall paintings.

# Under the Volcano at a Glance

The ideal time to visit here is in **spring** or **autumn**, before the searing heat and the crowds of **summer** appear, but it is still possible to visit at any time of year. If you are planning to climb Mount Vesuvius, it is best to do it early in the morning or late in the afternoon, when the light is better and the temperature kinder. Allow at least a full day to explore the area; preferably one day for Vesuvius and Herculaneum, a second full day for Pompeii.

The privately operated Circumvesuviana **train** (tel: 800 053 939, www.vesuvi ana.it) runs around the bay, from Naples to Sorrento, with stops both at Ercolano, for Herculaneum and Vesuvius and Pompeii-Scavi-Villa dei Misteri station for Pompeii. Beyond Pompeii, the line branches and you may have to change trains at Torre Annunziata or wait for the correct service to get back to Sorrento. You can get a city **bus** (Giranapoli tickets acceptable) if travelling from Naples to Ercolano. If **driving**, always park in paid areas.

*Vesuvius*
Infrequent buses head up the mountain from Erculano-Scavi station, but it is far easier and not much more expensive to use one of the shared taxis in the station forecourt. They will wait for you up top. From the car park near the summit, there's a 600m (197ft) climb up to the crater rim. Wear stout comfortable shoes, and take a hat and something to drink; www.parconazionaledel vesuvio.it/grancono/index.asp

*Ercolano*
The town buses stop beside the gates of the excavation; if coming from the station, walk downhill for about 300m (98ft). Open daily 09:00 until two hours before dusk, tel: 081 739 0963.

*Pompeii*
The main entrance is about 200m (66ft) from Pompeii Scavi–Villa dei Misteri sta-tion. Pompeii Town station is a long walk from the site, and if you leave by the Porta di Nocera at the far end of the site, you face a 2km (1-mile) walk back to the station, with no buses or taxis in sight. Open daily 09:00 until one hour before dusk. For admis-sion, tel: 081 861 0744.

It is better to stay in one of the wide range of hotels in Naples, Sorrento, the islands or Amalfi, rather than in this area. But is you wish to stay here, try:
*BUDGET*
**Certe Notti**, Via Nolana 128, Pompeii, tel: 081 863 6667, www.bebcertenotti. com Cheerful B&B about 300m from the ruins, offering spacious mini-apartments at cheap prices, shady gardens, free bikes for country rambles.
**Motel Villa dei Misteri**, Via Villa dei Misteri 11, Pompeii, tel: 081 861 3593, fax: 081 862 2983, www.villadei misteri.it Cheerful small hotel about 100m (110yd) from station and main entrance to the excavations.

**La Locanda di Annagrazia**, Via Colle S. Bartolomeo 71, Pompeii, tel: 081 863 2505. An attractively decorated country restaurant with friendly service, traditional Neapolitan food, and wine grown on the slopes of Mount Vesuvius.
**Il Principe**, Piazza Bartolo Longo, 1, Pompei, tel: 081 850 5566, www.ilprincipe. com With a background that includes service in hotels such as London's Savoy, the team behind this exclusive restaurant have cooked – and continue to cook – for presi-dents and kings, serving *haute cuisine* which marries local tradition with that of ancient Rome in the most elegant of surroundings. Very expensive. Book ahead.

*Tourist Information*
*Pompeii Town*
www.pompeiturismo.it
Via Sacra 1, Cap 80045, tel: 081 850 7255, fax: 081 863 2401.
**Pompeii Scavi**, Piazza Esedra 2.

# 5
# The Islands

Italy is blessedly fortunate in the number and variety of its islands, from the exotic Borromean Isles in Lake Maggiore to Stromboli off Sicily and Murano and Burano ghostly in the misty Venetian lagoon, they are many and magnificent. Yet perhaps the most famous are the isles lying off the coast of Campania. These three are particularly renowned, and have been since Classical times. In love with their beauties, Roman aristocrats staked claims on these rocky retreats, set like green, white and gold gems in a shimmering sea. These early cultured visitors left many relics, so an additional pleasure is the discovery of many antique sites as you explore. For centuries since then, they have been the destination for the artistic, the flamboyant, and the rich. Famed throughout the world, they are Ischia, Prócida and the best known of all, Capri.

You really shouldn't leave Campania without taking the short journey to these exotic spots. The voyage across an aquamarine sea to experience their breathtaking loveliness is in itself a dream. If **Capri** seems too commercial and crowded (which, alas, it often is) then try the larger and equally fascinating **Ischia**, or closer in to Naples and the mainland, the quiet and little-explored charms of **Prócida**. These two islands will indeed give you a better impression of how people live than the much more international Capri. All three islands are easy to get to on fast and frequent ferries and hydrofoils. Once at the quaysides you have a choice of many pleasures from tours or walks, or just sitting at the cafés and watching life go by.

## DON'T MISS

**\*\*\* The Blue Grotto:** reflected light from the waters illumines this famous cave.
**\*\* Villa Jove, Capri:** a series of sites where a Roman emperor ended a life of luxury.
**\*\* Villa San Michele, Anacapri:** a splendid house with antique treasures, gardens and loggias with views.
**\*\* Hot springs on Ischia:** take a cure by bathing in the hot pools, or simply visit the many spas of this island
**\*\* Prócida:** the smallest island with multicoloured houses overlooking the sea.

**Opposite:** *A popular nature walk on Capri takes you to the Natural Arch.*

## TALE OF TWO EMPERORS

The emperors **Augustus** and **Tiberius** lived here. Augustus visited, built a villa and founded the gardens named after him. Tiberius lived the last 10 years of his life here (AD27–37). He moved his entire court to Capri, ruling his far flung empire from the Villa. The stories of his pleasures and orgies were a scandal, even in decadent Rome. It appears that this enticing island has always had a lure for those in search of excess – inspiration too. Certainly artists and writers still come here in droves.

**Below:** *Boats and ferries dock at the Marina Grande, the lively harbour on Capri.*

## CAPRI

If you have wondered why a tiny place like Capri, only 6km (4 miles) long, has always been considered one of the ultimate holiday settings for sensation seekers, then all one can say is 'try it'. This is without doubt one of the most delectable destinations in the Mediterranean, if not the world. Butting up from azure seas, the small cliff-walled isle really is alluring. Once attached to the long craggy arm of the Sorrentine Peninsula, this final separated piece of the mainland is spectacular, be it views of beetling cliff, rugged white rocks, limestone caves, tiny sand beaches, or pretty towns, all framed by a brilliant sea. It offers so much for romantics as well as hedonistic sun and sea lovers. Its picturesque settlements have good restaurants, sun-splashed cafés and lots of smart little shops set along narrow atmospheric streets. If you want to do more than just flop on a café chair, bask on a sandy spit, or swim in a clear warm bay, then go on a boat trip or take a stroll. Longer walks in the country along well marked paths will take you around the island and along the cliffs for a series of splendid views.

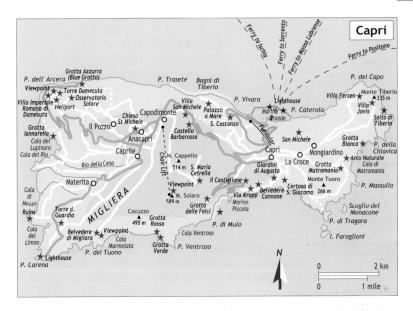

Capri offers a constant kaleidoscope of scenery. Heavenly scents rise from flowers, which are everywhere, or from herbs crushed underfoot. As the afternoon wears on lemons glow in their trees as a big red sun sets over the sea. To visit here is to experience sheer joy.

## CAPRI TOWN

Boats dock at the **Marina Grande** on the north side of the island. It's a pretty seaside town, and as the main port and fishing centre, offers good seafood restaurants. From here, it's a steep walk or funicular ride up to the town of **Capri** that spreads itself along the neck of the island, between the two main hills, **Monte Tiberio** and **Monte Solaro**. In the 16th century, with the area troubled by pirates, the town slowly moved back from the sea to the col it now occupies, where the inhabitants could live in relative safety. Capri town centres around the **Piazza Umberto I**, known as the Piazzetta, a square filled with cafés and restaurants, abuzz with chat and social activity from dawn til dusk.

### WALKS

Try going on foot in Capri. It is possible to walk on shore-looping paths and up to the heights of Anacapri. Paths are well kept and marked. Strolling at an agreeable pace, you will get scenic views, perhaps catch sights of Capri's wildlife, picnic, or pause at a beach for a swim. Go east to the **Villa Jovis** (Jupiter's Villa), where the entire island can be seen from the terrace. It was here that Tiberius lived, and when enraged, had his victims thrown down the cliff called, **Salto di Tiberio**. Go up to the **Arco Naturale**, to find the imposing palace built on Capri by the Emperor. Allow at least half an hour to climb up from the town.

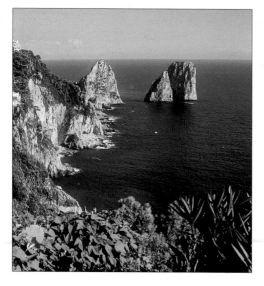

**Above:** *The Faraglioni are three massive limestone rocks that rise out of the ocean at about 107m (350ft), just off the coast of Capri.*

## Things to See

Take a lazy stroll along the narrow, flower-hung passages and alleys of the medieval quarter to the **Certosa di San Giacomo**, a 14th-century Carthusian monastery. Within this simple white church and cloister is a gallery of 17th–19th-century paintings. Not far off, the **Belvedere Cannone** sits above glorious views along the cliffs. Below the gardens of the **Giardini di Augusto** offer flowers and shade. The steeply down-dipping **Via Krupp**, plummets down around sharp curves and turns to arrive at the sea and the **Marina Piccola**. Once a fishing village, it now has water sports and beach pleasures.

Capri is indeed enchanting, full of elegant shops and galleries too, but in summer it gets cruelly crowded. Visitors arrive on every boat and the town is completely submerged in a sea of day-trippers. Even so, you can still get away, especially on walks. Or go out of season, stop over in one of the isle's small hotels and you will have quite a different experience.

After you have explored Capri town, head back down to the Marina Grande, and take to the water for a boat tour around the rest of the island. One tour will take you to the dramatic group of rocks south of the island called the **Faraglioni**, but the most sought after is a trip round to the **Grotta Azzurra** (Blue Grotto). This is one of the many flooded caverns found here, but thanks to its extraordinary lighting conditions, it is one of the most spectacular grottoes to be found anywhere. Entered by small rowing boat, it is quite an experience. The craft is propelled by boatmen as it negotiates the

### LOCAL LIFE

Join in with the smart, yet informal local life of the island. Take coffee, a drink, dinner under the stars, followed by a lazy stroll through Capri's **Piazza Umberto 1** or along one of the island's quays, especially when a ferryboat comes in. It's always lively with social causerie, sentimental music and song, until late. The life of the town can be greatly enjoyed here.

narrow entry with its foam and whirl of water. Inside, the enormous high roofed cave presents a sudden calm and the illuminated walls are indeed a ghostly, luminous blue, as light shimmers up in vivid reflections from the pale sand below the water. The visit can be short, but if you are adventurous you can swim in, except wait till the press of boats has decreased as they head home.

Also on Capri are other caverns. At the **Grotta Matromania**, the Romans had a shrine to Cybele. Nearby is the **Arco Naturale**, a huge sea carved stone arch.

## ANACAPRI

High up the hill, Anacapri is a pleasing little town, with a detailed scale model of the island in the main square. A bus trip saves you a hard walk (the Scala Fenicia has nearly 800 steps so you need to be energetic). You will be rewarded after the climb with wonderful views to the sea and harbour. Pause, take a refreshing drink, or explore the spectacularly sited Villa San Michele.

In the town centre, the **Church of San Michele** has a majolica pavement of the 18th century representing the Garden of Eden. A few minutes' walk away the simple

**Below:** *The Via Krupp on Capri, an impressive road winding its way to the sea.*

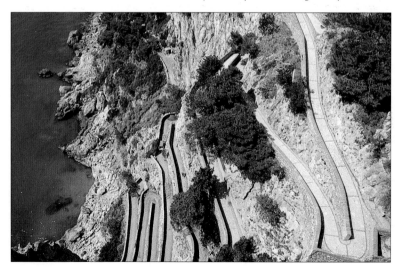

**Below:** *Take a chairlift up to Monte Solaro, and admire the magnificent views of Anacapri, the only other town on the island.*

Scandinavian design of the Villa San Michele is a stunning contrast to its exotic setting. It was built by Dr. Axel Munthe, a 19th-century Swedish scientist, who wrote a popular book entitled *The Story of San Michele,* about living on the island. As well as the cool, elegant villa itself, he enjoyed creating an enchanting classic Italian garden with spacious loggias and pools. The views of the sea and isle from the pergola perched at the end of the garden above the Scala Fenicia, are amazing. In the house are examples of Italian and Swedish antiques, family mementos and Roman remains found in the gardens.

From the Piazza Vittoria, take a chair lift to the summit of **Monte Solaro,** which at 589m (1930ft) is the highest point on the island. The views across the entire Bay of Naples are superb. Far below, a small fleet of boats ferries hundreds of tourists around on trips or through narrow cliff openings to visit the Grottoes.

## ISCHIA

Although Capri is famous there are those who prefer a less renowned place, and find Ischia best of the trio of alluring islands. To begin with there is more space. At

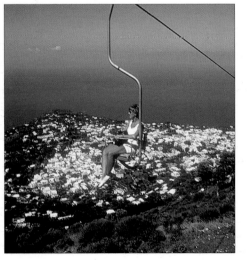

70km² (27 sq miles), Ischia is the largest of the three, furthest out to sea, and opposite Capri. It may be less famous and less visited than the idyllic island of Capri (although very popular among the Germans), but Ischia is not second rate. It is a place for the discerning, deserving a special trip, as its scenery is beautifully varied, and its coast cut with creeks and bays. Formed by volcanic eruptions, you are often reminded that its fiery origins took place not so long ago, for there are hot springs everywhere. Its central volcanic mountains stand out against the serene sky, and from beneath these ancient peaks the thermal springs leap up, their super-heated water forced from deep underground boilers. There are establishments that provide bathing cures wherever these sulphurous springs pop up, or as they run down to sandy beaches. Unfortunately this island that the Romans loved became a mass market destination some time ago, but this hasn't yet obliterated Ischia's charm.

There are many small quaint villages. The main town is **Ischia Porto**, which is also the ferry port, an old volcanic crater. With neighbouring **Ischia Ponte** this pleasant town has good sandy beaches. There are many facilities where people can try its radioactive volcanic springs. Indeed a substantial number of visitors come to try cures for sufferers of a host of varied ailments. Ischia Ponte, is actually older and named after a dyke connecting it to an imposing fort, the photogenic and part ruined **Castello Aragonese**. This short causeway conducts you to the one-time Aragonese stronghold on its small islet, surrounded by pinewoods and churches.

The presence of hot springs is a major lure for visitors to Ischia's other coastal resort towns. These include **Casamicciola Terme**, **Spiaggia di Citara** and **Sant'Angelo**, possessing springs, beaches, large hotels and a lot of commercial holiday attractions. **Forio** in particular strives to add its own appeal with historic features from small churches to frowning town walls. For those interested in the island's history, nearby **Lacco Ameno** of Greek origin, has a museum of archaeology within the **Villa Arbusto**, an 18th-century

**Above:** *The enchanting Villa San Michele, Capri.*

### WALTON'S RETREAT

For many years, the composer **William Walton**, perhaps best known for his music for films, lived a quiet life here. Knighted for his music, he chose **Ischia** as his retreat. Since the Grand Tour, many wealthy English settlers and amateur gardeners lived in Italy, attracted partly by the warmth, flowers and exotic shrubs. He and Lady Walton created a charming garden here that can be visited. You can also stay here.

**Ischia**

P. Cornácchia
Latco
Ameno —Casamicciola
Montevergine    Terme    Hot Spring
          Villa Arbusto    Perrone    Lighthouse
Spinesante    Fango    Bagni
  Forio    Monterone    Maio    Ischia
          M. Epomeo              Ischia
          ▲★ Viewpoint           Ponte
  S270    Pietra 788 m    Fiaiano    Sant'    Castello
          dell'Acqua           Antuono Aragonese
Spiaggia    721 m Fontana    Piedimonte
di Citara ○ Cuotto    Noia ○ ★ Viewpoint    Campagnano
Hot Spring    ★           Buonopane    Molara
  ★ Battaglia    Serrara    Barano ○ ▲ M. di Vezzi
Lighthouse    Fontana    d'Ischia    394 m
  Panza    Terme
          Cavascura    Testáccio
  Succhivo ○    Lido di Maronti    P. San Pancrazio
Fumarole Hot Spring ○    Maronti
    Sant'Angelo    Beach
        P. Sant'Angelo
          0        2 km
                          Bocca Grande
          0      1 mile

N

Ferry to Naples and Pozzuoli
Ferry to Capri
Ferry to Sorrento

mansion. Sant'Angelo, benefits in picturesque aspects from its position on a narrow isthmus and tiny isle. It is set in the southern part with steep hills falling to the shore. There are more thermal springs to be found at **Terme Cavascura**, and an impressive natural steam vent, the Fumarole, voids here. From Fontana, a short distance away, it is a stiff hour-long walk up to the summit of the island's highest mountain, **Monte Epomeo** at 788m (2585ft), from where there are vast panoramic views. If you don't want to get footsore you can ride up the mountain on donkeys.

## PRÓCIDA

Less visited than Ischia, and often overlooked, take time for a day trip to little Prócida, which is a fascinating place and still relatively unspoilt. You may be quite charmed by it, however, so don't restrict your visit. It is appealing to walkers too, with a chance to spot animal, bird and insect life along its paths and lanes. Lying beside Prócida, a narrow fingernail of land linked by a bridge, takes you to the **Isolotto di Vivara**. You will need to apply to visit this nature reserve.

Prócida is quite tiny at 4km (2.5 miles) long. It is an island of ancient volcanic origin, with its once high craters long smoothed and broken down by erosion. This intriguing yet simple island offers the visitor that rare thing, a part of Campania that is not overrun with tourists. Like Ischia, it is part of the Campi Flegrei, created in the Tertiary era on a volcanic extension, and seated on ancient lava flows. Along with being the smallest, it is least developed of the three islands. It is blessedly much freer of the allure of tourist money, so expect simplicity. As you move around you will note a more prosperous past as reflected in its many old crumbling villas. Its present day houses are bright and charming, white or colour-washed and often domed, connected with arcades, terraces, and outdoor stair-cases. They are still lived in for the most part by fisher families, gardeners and wine growers. (Ask to try local wines at cafés or bars.) Everywhere Prócida presents a simple, older lifestyle, its quiet aspect marking it as a charming and as yet undiscovered place.

**Chiaiolella**, at the end of the island, has good beaches. They are reached past painted houses with terraced gardens, through colourful fishing villages with their boats and cottages set against vines, citrus and olive trees. Here you can feel like a local as you sit in the sun, or swim from uncrowded beaches and eat on the terraces of simple trattoria. Regular ferries dock at the main town of **Marina di Sancio Cattolico** (commonly called the Marina Grande) with its narrow streets that plunge down from the 16th-century **Castello**. Like so many fortified castles in Italy, this was until recently, used as a prison. Stroll through the **Terra Murata** (Walled Town). Also at Terra Murata is the charm-ing **Certosa di San Michele Arcangelo** (Monastery of the Arch-angel Michael), its principal treasure a painting from the Nea-politan School. Luca Giordano was one of Caravaggio's more original pupils. This picture is of the arch-angel, supposedly pre-venting the invasion of Prócida from the Turks.

**Below:** *Lemon trees in Prócida. The overwhelm-ing scent of lemons pervades the entire Bay of Naples – they grow every-where and are used for everything from perfume to the local speciality liqueur, limoncello.*

# The Islands at a Glance

The lure of Capri and the islands is the almost constant **mild weather** in the Bay of Naples. It is rarely cold or dank, although you may expect occasional rain in **spring** and **autumn**. Even in **winter** the sun shines; although it's too cool to sunbathe it is frost free, so the foliage and flowers continue. It is pleasingly warm in spring and autumn. Very busy in the **hot summer** months, however.

Capri offers lovely **walks**, and Ischia, though less compact, also has well marked paths. The views from special points along the routes are splendid. To get around short island distances, **taxis** are much in evidence. Local **bus** lines also ascend the hills and make fairly frequent connections. Bus tickets can be purchased from newsagents; take detailed maps if you are hiking. The islands are connected by **ferry boats** (and some hydrofoils) There are frequent sailings between islands and to Naples.

## Capri
### LUXURY
**Villa Brunella**, Via Tragara 24, tel: 081 837 0122, brunella@ mbox.caprinet.it www.villa brunella.it If you prefer the comforts of a modern hotel, built on a steeply terraced

slope among the lemon groves, and don't mind lots of steps, this is a great place. The hotel has 20 rooms, sea views and a swimming pool. Seasonal opening.
**La Scalinatella**, Via Tragara 10, Capri 80073, tel: 081 837 0633, www.scalinatella.com This smart little place is made up of two villas containing, of all things, an array of oriental furniture. All 20 bedrooms are suites, and have jacuzzis and ornate balconies with views. Have lunch by the pool and sop up the atmosphere as well as the succulent food.
**Grand Hotel Quisisana**, Via Camarelle 2, Capri, 80073, tel: 081 837 0788, www.quisi sana.com This is without doubt a place for those with bottomless resources – very expensive and very luxurious, it has two top class restaurants and marvellous views. It is hard to believe that this large ochre-coloured hotel was actually a sanitorium when it first opened in the 1840s.

### MID-RANGE
**Villa Sarah**, Via Tiberio 3/A, tel: 081 837 7817, www. villasarahcapri.com Just outside Capri Town, this 20-room hotel stands in vineyards. Gardens surround the peaceful white painted house.

### BUDGET
**Villa Krupp**, Via Matteoti 12, tel: 081 837 0362, www. villakrupp.it On the cliff with

a view down to the Marina Piccola, this is a historic villa. Both Lenin and Gorki made it their home – though not as a couple! There are 12 rooms and a simple air at this quaint family run place. Seasonal opening.
**Lotus Flower**, Via Rio Linciano 65, Anacapri, tel: 081 837 2635, www.lotus flower.hostel.com A tiny B&B in Anacapri with friendly hosts, comfortable rooms and a garden for lazing in away from the overwhelming glitz of Capri Town.

## Ischia
### LUXURY
**Mezzatorre**, Località San Montano Nord Forio, tel: 081 986 111, www.mezzatorre.it Not a monastery this time, but a Saracen tower which was once home to Luigi Visconti, the film director. The hotel is built around the old fortification among pines at the northern end of San Montano Bay, just two miles from Forio. A terrace, seawater pool, spa and gardens. Seasonal opening.

### MID-RANGE
**Il Monastero**, Castello Aragonese Ischia Ponte, tel: 081 992 435, www. albergoilmonastero.it Simple and plain rooms in a converted monastery. Situated within castle walls and with great views, makes this hotel more than just a bargain.

**La Villarosa**, Via Giacinto Gigante 5, Ischia Porto, tel: 081 991 316, www.dico hotels.it This 37-room hotel is a good choice in the centre of town. Luxury at a reasonable price with 19th-century antiquities and charm. Open Apr–Oct, it has a spa and there is a swimming pool within its pleasant gardens.

### WHERE TO EAT

### Capri
*LUXURY*
**Da Paolino**, Via Palazzo a Mare 11 Marina Grande, tel: 081 837 6102, www.paolino capri.com Set amidst groves of citrus fruits, this is a charming and popular place to eat. Specialities are grilled local fish and desserts.
**Le Canzone del Mare**, Via Marina Piccola 93, Marina Piccola, tel: 081 837 0104, www.lacanzonedelmare.com Quite a grand place, much enjoyed by well-off locals, as well as rich settlers. There is a terrace where you can have a drink; the food is excellent.
**Il Riccio**, Via Gradula 4, Grotta Azzurra, Tel: 081 837 1380, www.ristoranteilriccio. com A historic restaurant at the foot of the cliff near the Blue Grotto recently revamped into a stylish beach club, cocktail bar and seafood restaurant.

*MID-RANGE*
**Aurora**, Via Fuorlovado 18, tel: 081 837 0181, www.

auroracapri.com One of those places wallpapered with pictures of celebrities who may have dropped by. A justifiably popular and long-established pizzeria. Closed winters.
**Da Gemma**, Via Madre Serafina, tel: 081 837 0461, www.dagemma.it Could appear rather old style and maybe a bit kitsch yet this is a lovely, friendly trattoria. If you don't like the copper pans and pottery, enjoy the very good pasta and pizza. Open all year.

### Ischia
*LUXURY*
**Damiano**, Via Nuova Circumvallazione Ischia Porto, tel: 081 983 032. Beautiful views of the old port from here, you are high up and can see for miles. The accent is on seafood, and the wines are mostly local or southern. Dinner every evening, except Sun. Seasonal opening.

*MID-RANGE*
**Lo Scoglio**, Via Cava Ruffano, Sant'Angelo, tel: 081 999 529. Large portions of traditional home-cooked island food and a spectacular setting, the restaurant literally carved into the sea cliff.

### Prócida
Being less of a tourist destination than Capri and Ischia, there are fewer hotels in

Prócida and it is often considered to be a mere day excursion from Naples. However, you can stay and eat very well on this small compact island.

### SHOPPING

The islands have lots of small shops in the town centres offering an array of souvenirs, clothes and local handicrafts. Capri in particular also has a number of fashion boutiques and shops selling luxury goods and jewellery. Street markets offer bargains in local produce.

### TOURS AND EXCURSIONS

Visits to local attractions are all expertly catered for from ancient sites and grottoes with coach and walking guided tours. Check Tourist Offices for many possibilities.

### USEFUL CONTACTS

*Tourist Offices*
*Capri*
Azienda Autonoma di Cura Soggiorno e Turismo, Piazzetta I. Cerio 11, Capri, tel: 081 837 5308, touristoffice@capri.it www.capritourism.com

*Ischia*
via Sogliuzzo 72, Ischia Porto, tel: 081 507 4211, www.infoischiaprocida.it

*Anacapri*
Via G. Orlandi 59, tel: 081 837 1524.

# 6
# The Sorrento Peninsula

Like a lover from Greek classic tales, the two arms of the Bay of Naples embrace the Mediterranean Sea. They extend from the city around the blue of the bay to form a naturally protected harbour. While the northern arm, stretching from Pozzuoli to Ischia and Prócida, is the result of volcanic action, the southern is mainly limestone, its white and grey rocks marking one of the few non-volcanic areas around the bay. This is the spectacularly beautiful and renowned **Peninsula Sorrentina**, a land mass extending to Capri, which is divided from the mainland by a channel called **Bocca Piccola** at its end. This chapter deals with the northwest facing shore of the peninsula. On the other side is the long Amalfi Drive (see Chapter 7).

This extended natural breakwater of rock is moored firmly to the mainland shore. It offers a remarkable tour, with renowned villages clinging to cliffs and hills from Stabio to Sorrento. Drive along over 32km (20 miles) of unparalleled beauty, slowly, for the road loops and dips around the shores and edges a rugged land. There are masses of lovely wild flowers and herbs, rocks cushioned with long lush green grasses, fruitful orange and lemon groves, gnarled olives trees and sweeping draperies of vines. All around is the sea, indescribably blue, clear and brilliant. Hovering like a shadow in the background, ever present against the seductive Italian skies is the all too real Mount Vesuvius, her only flag of possible danger the very occasional soft ascending feather of smoke.

### DON'T MISS

*** The whole **Sorrento** drive is a top sight in every way, with lovely constantly changing views.
*** Stop and admire the many **gardens** along the drive, especially in Sorrento.
** **Punte del Capo di Sorrento:** walk the headland on a well-made path for wonderful views to Sorrento.
** The **Lattari mountains** are the backbone of the peninsula, and **Sant'Agata sui due Golfi** has splendid views to the north and south.

**Opposite:** *Take a pleasant walk around Sorrento, with views of the Bay of Naples.*

## THE PASSING OF PLINY

One of the most touching stories of the exploding **Vesuvius** was that of a naturalist, who on hearing news of the eruption, hurried here on a boat to record the eruption and observe it at closer range. It was not a wise decision. The Roman scientist came too close to the clouds of superheated gas, and professional interest resulted in the death of Pliny the Elder by **asphyxiation**.

**Below:** *The enchanting resort town of Sorrento is packed with tourists in summer owing to its great location and mild climate.*

## CASTELLAMMARE DI STABIA

Your trip along the famous peninsula of Sorrento starts south east of Naples at Castellammare di Stabia. This is Italy's main naval base and a thermal resort too; there are no fewer than 28 springs and treatments at the **Antiche Terme**. In Classical times it was the spa town of Stabiae and has a very long and varied history going back to the Oscans – who were there even before the Etruscans. Rome took over in the 4th century BC and the town was later rebuilt in an unusual design – a new town of connected houses with villas in the country-side. A neighbour of Pompeii, it too vanished in the great eruption of AD79. The local museum, the Antiquarium, has relics, frescoes, stucco reliefs and sculptures salvaged from Roman buildings of the town. Nearby, several villas that once faced Vesuvius and were buried, have now been excavated. The two-storey **Villa San Marco** had gardens and swimming pools and even today on a visit you can imagine the luxury of the Roman life of the time, along with the well

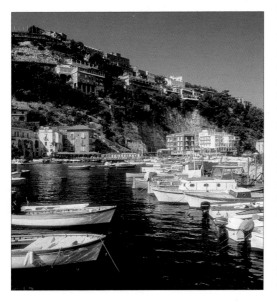

restored **Villa di Arianna**. They are both about 2km (1 mile) from the present town. The port of Castellammare was revived and repaired in the 18th century and is a working harbour and shipyard today.

You will want to take time to see the spectacular views of sea and rocky shore, but if not there is a faster road to Sorrento by the coast (with some tunnels), from Naples, avoiding Castellammare. The S269, running from the edges of Castellammare

Sorrento Peninsula

is an adventurous trip, however. The drive up the upper slopes of **Monte Faito** offers wonderful vistas, but the road is a cluster of hairpin bends. As you leave the town, turn left to head up Monte Faito, part of the jagged limestone range of the Lattari mountains. This is the high ground that separates the Bay from the Gulf of Salerno. (If you have no car, then take the cable car from Castellammare station up the mountain for an overall view.) The road loops and dips dramatically to hit the height and then narrows down to **Vico Equense** through woods. On the way you should stop at several viewpoints for wide panoramas of the Bay of Naples. **Vico**, on the mouth of the River d'Arco, is a small health resort in a pretty rocky setting.

You will also see many vine terraces. For protection against frost, citrus trees are masked with matting in winter, their tender shoots sheltered beneath the covered vine trellises. The drive is most memorable in spring, when many of Italy's wild flowers are in bloom, adding a seductive beauty, while budding new leaves of herbs scent the warm air. On warm days you can also hear the beautiful sounds of birds singing and insects calling.

### VIEWS AND MORE VIEWS

Along the steep mountain road there are several places to stop – with parking. The first you arrive at is **Belvedere del Capi** with a wide view of the Bay of Naples. Further up you come to **Cappella San Michele** with an even wider panorama. The contrast between the mountain scenery and the view below is marked. The climb up is heavily wooded, with many fine beech trees from which the mountain takes its name.

## POETIC HERO

The Piazza Tasso was named after the poet, **Torquato Tasso**, who was born in Sorrento in 1544. He travelled several times to the glittering court of Ferrara to court fame, and elsewhere in the north to enjoy the support of the cultivated Este family. There, he wrote the epic poem for which he is most famous, **Gerusalleme Liberata**, in which Jerusalem is won by Christians. Threaded through the poem is the love story of Rinaldo and Armida. See the statue of Tasso on the square.

**Below:** *The Piazza Tasso, situated in the centre of Sorrento.*

## SORRENTO

Next along this lovely shore comes Sorrento, overlooking its Gulf with views across an azure and violet sea to Capri. Rightly famed as a remarkable resort, it is a perfect place to indulge yourself, to stay or just stop and eat, even if you are only passing through. As the principal town of the peninsula ranged along its clifftop, with terraces and ledges, and a scattering of lovely gardens, this resort town has been a place people have come to visit for the last 2500 years. It preserves an air of another era and it is easy to picture late 19th-century visitors playing croquet, or demurely using bathing machines in the sea below, where now modern swimming quays stick out like decks. Sorrento has remained a lovely, stylish, and grand, if somewhat faded place. Despite its popularity, the town has not succumbed to too much commercial adjustment and remains a year-round resort with sophisticated facilities for tourists. Visitors will find a town that is elegant, well organized and a centre for road, rail and boat connections. It has hotels, inns and many pensiones not to mention cafés, bars and excellent restaurants where you can often eat on terraces to

Sorrento map showing Golfo di Napoli, Marina Grande, Marina Piccola, Piazza Tasso, Duomo, Chiesa di San Francesco, Museo Correale di Terranova, Railway Station, Corso Italia, and surrounding streets. Scale 0–400 m / 0–400 yd. N arrow.

enjoy the warm air. The foliage framing the town is rich and varied from the dark leaves and brilliant gold fruits of the many citrus groves, to exotic shrubs, while colourful flowers embower many houses. Even winter can hardly dull this glorious display.

Sorrento has but one museum, the **Museo Correale di Terranova**. This pretty 17th-century villa houses an old fashioned jumble of all sorts of things, from statuary to a notable collection of 17th–18th-century furniture, china and glass. There are mementos of the town's poet, Tasso, and a terrace with fine views.

This long narrow town is best for sauntering through streets and passages enjoying the wide range of local life at restaurants and cafés spilling onto the pavements. At the foot of the town the old fishing port, the **Marina Grande**, is lively too, while the ferry port in the **Marina Piccola** provides many connections to Naples, Capri, Ischia and several other coastal towns.

Directly above the ferry dock is the centre of the town and the **Piazza Tasso**, honouring Sorrento's 16th-century poet. Along **Corso Italia** you can explore the 18th-century **Palazzo Correale**, with a fine majolica courtyard, and go into the 15th-century **Duomo** (cathedral). Of the other churches, look for the tall belfry of the most interesting, the **Chiesa di San Francesco** (Church of St Francis). It appears Baroque but explore further, for later additions hide a pretty cloister with intertwined stone arches, its charming capitals carved with leaves, in a 13th-century Sicilian-Arabic style.

## STAYING IN SPLENDOUR

Sorrento possesses some **lavish hotels** in *belle époque* style. They exude an elegance and a sophistication that is second to none. Italy's luxurious top hotels, or *grandi alberghi*, offer the best service in the world, whatever the Swiss may say! The **food** often uses local products, for example sauces are heightened and made piquant with the juice of local lemons.

## MARQUETRY

Among other local handi-works there is a long-lived local trade in the making of **marquetry**, or **intarsia** works. These objects of intricately inlaid woods, some of them rare and precious, come in many forms, from boxes and trays to quite large pieces of furniture and elaborate pictures. Whether they appeal or not, they are yet another facet of that ever-inventive Italian flair for clever artistry in amazingly detailed works.

## Touring the Villages

A long walk can encompass several of the pretty villages in the rocky countryside around the town. You will find some settlements such as **Sant'Agnello** and **Meta di Sorrento**, home to the 18th-century Bourbon shipyards, very close by and effectively now residential suburbs. If you are up to a very long walk and frequent climbs, around 32km (20 miles), follow the car route. You can do half of it around **Pico Sant'Angelo** by ascending the S145 over the hills and heading down towards the Amalfi Coast and Sant'Agata. Standing high on the ridge of the Lattari mountains, which form the backbone of the peninsula, **Sant'Agata sui due Golfi** has superb views to the north and south, over two gulfs, as its name suggests. One is the Bay of Naples, and in the other direction, over the Amalfi Coast you see the Bay of Salerno. On the way back pass through **Colli di San Pietro** then up towards **Piano di Sorrento**, which has a thriving market on Monday mornings. **Meta** has a noteworthy church, the **Basilica Santa Maria del Lauro**. For a real hike head from Sorrento towards the far end of the Penisola Sorrentina where you will find in high, dry hills, with exotic plants and cacti, a scattering of about 30 small hamlets known collectively as the **Massa Lubrense**. They are well hidden among breathtakingly lovely scenery with excellent walks and superb views of the Bay across to Capri.

## ARTISTIC INSPIRATION

The coast has always attracted **painters** of all sorts and you will often see artists at work intent on capturing the ravishing scenes. There are small **galleries** too, showing images of this area in all sorts of media. Of course you can buy if you feel so inclined, and an original picture makes a good souvenir, but take time when making a selection.

## Circular Drive

The road that circles the end of the peninsula, the S145, traverses a marvel of scenery with wooded hillside views and is a short distance, but can take much longer if you have the time. You can amble along slowly and easily spend a day, taking many pauses and perhaps even having a picnic on the heights. (As already noted, it should be walked by those who have brought the right footwear and clothes, for the hills are quite steep.) A winding road bisects the route across the loop of the shore-hugging S145, so it can be

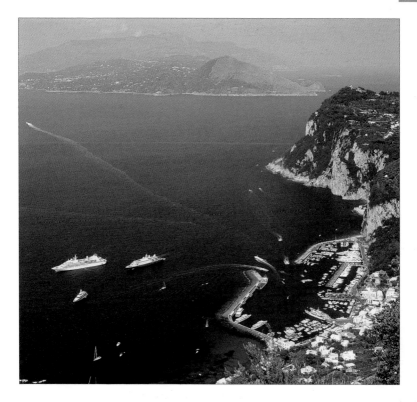

shortened. Start westwards from Sorrento on the S145. At the high point of the cliffy shoreline, **Capo di Sorrento** should be visited – a road conducts you to the headland. At the village of Capo beside the church, you will have to walk, so allow time. You will be rewarded with a thrilling view back to Sorrento.

Continue down the peninsula to Massa Lubrense and the final height of the tongue of land, **Monte San Costanzo**. The south-facing shore offers visits to **Marina dei Cantone** on the sea and **Sant'Agata**. The road dips steeply to **Colli di San Pietro**.

Return on the S163, which offers wonderful views to the Bay of Naples on its descent before you arrive back in Sorrento.

**Above:** *Sorrento Peninsula with Capri in the distance.*

## Sorrento at a Glance

Sorrento is a year-round destination with lovely warm weather during **spring** and **autumn**. Like much of this part of the coast, it can get very crowded in **summer**. It is popular with people escaping northern chills in **winter**, when it is mild and frost-free here.

The best and most attractive way to get to Sorrento is by **boat**, and the town has a lively port with a well-ordered system of sailing. Sorrento is connected by frequent **ferry** and **hydrofoil** to Naples (Beverello and Mergellina), the islands and, infrequently, the Amalfi Coast; for contacts of ferry companies, see Travel Tips, p. 123. If travelling by **bus** from Naples, and once in Sorrento, try the blue SITA buses which run to nearby villages, as well as to Positano and Amalfi. Buses leave from the station. Tickets can be bought from newsagents. Direct coach services to and from Rome. For **air** connections Autolinee Curreri Service operate a direct bus service to Capodichino Airport four times daily, leaving from Piazza Tasso. For information, tel: 081 801 5420. If travelling by **train**, Sorrento is on the Circumvesuviana line (tel: 800 053 939, www.vesuviana.it), which includes stops at Pompeii, Ercolano and Naples. When returning, check that you are on the Sorrento section as the line forks.

It's easy to **walk** but **taxis** are not a problem, tel Sorrento: 081 878 2204 or Sant'Agnello: 081 878 1428. The Syrenbus (tel: 081 807 4220) is a **limousine** service for transfers and sightseeing. Local orange **buses**, operated by Severzio Autolinee, serve the town, including the Marina Grande, Marina Piccola, the station and Piazza Tasso en route.

### Sorrento
*LUXURY*
**Bellevue Syrene**, Piazza della Vittoria 5, tel: 081 878 1024, www.bellevue.it Old, grand clifftop hotel built in 1750, and once favoured by parvenu empress Eugénie in the opulent 19th century. Antiques, paintings, a Pompeiian restaurant. Nice gardens and terraces.
**Grand Hotel Excelsior Vittoria**, Piazza T. Tasso 34, tel: 081 877 7111, cxvitt@exvitt.it www.exvitt.it This hotel has had many famous guests in its time. Decorations include frescoes and ceramics. Cliff-top terrace, gardens, lift down to the port, pool and restaurant.

*MID-RANGE*
**Royal**, Via Correale 42, tel: 081 807 3434, ghroyal@maniello hotels.it www.royalsorrento. com Old and charming clifftop hotel, very good service, within range of normal pockets. There are views of Vesuvius from terraces, a pool and gardens. Other hotels in the area under

the same management are the Ambasciatori, Capodimonte and Hotel de la Ville.
**Villa di Sorrento**, Piazza Tasso, tel: 081 878 1068, www.villa disorrento.it Centrally placed in town, this small hotel offers no views, and plain yet satisfactory rooms – an attractive medium-price option.

*BUDGET*
**Hotel Prestige Sorrento**, via Nastro Azzurro 23, tel: 081 533 0470, www.hotelprestige sorrento.com Perched on the hill above the main town with a free shuttle bus. Great views, helpful staff and excellent breakfasts; 25 rooms; no pool.
**Youth Hostel**, Via degli Aranci 60, tel: 081 807 2925.

### Outside Sorrento
**La Badia**, Via Nastro Verde 8, tel: 081 878 1154, www.hotel labadia.it Converted abbey set amidst olive and lemon groves on the hill just above Sorrento (on the bus route to the centre; 10 mins) with superb views over the town and bay. Attractively furnished, friendly, with a pool and restaurant.
**Capo la Gala**, Vico Equense. Via Luigi Serio 7, Capo la Gala, 80069, tel: 081 801 5758, www.hotelcapolagala.com Near-hidden, modern, 18-room hotel with pool; has a series of terraces down the cliff face. Economic rooms, but a welcoming air.
**Il Tulipano**, via Nastro Azzurro, 24, 80067 Sant'Agnello di Sorrento, tel: 081 808 3585,

# Sorrento at a Glance

www.iltulipanosorrento.com
About 5km from the centre of
Sorrento (easily reached by
bus), this small, friendly B&B
offers cosy affordable accommodation, lovely views and
peaceful surroundings.

**Crowne Plaza Hotel Stabiae**,
Hotel – SS 145 Sorrentina, Km
11, Localita' Pozzano, Castellammare di Stabia, tel: 081 394
6700, www.crowneplaza
sorrento.com A former factory
tucked between the road and
the coast converted into a very
sleek resort hotel with superb
food, a private beach and one
of the largest spas in Campania.

**Hotel Villa Pina**, Via Partenope
40, Massa Lubrense, tel: 081
533 9780, www.villapina.net
Terrace with views.

## WHERE TO EAT

*Sorrento*

**La Lanterna**, via San Cesareo
23, tel: 0818 781 355, www.
lalanternarestaurantsorrento.
com Set down a narrow sidestreet in Sorrento, with a shady
courtyard, a Roman hot springs
in the basement and a truly
impressive wine list, this is both
a lovely relaxed place for lunch
and a gourmet haven serving
luscious food.

**Trattoria da Emilia**, Via Marina
Grande 62, tel: 081 807 2720.
Family run, small yet has a
well-cooked range of fish and
pasta. It's popular as an authentic family-run trattoria by the
sea, with the old-style checked
cloths and candles in bottles.

**Tasso**, Via Correale 11d, tel:
081 878 5809, www.ristorante

tasso.com Sophisticated fish
and vegetable dishes, central.

**Il Buco**, Il Rampa Marina
Piccola, tel: 081 878 2354,
www.ilbucoristorante.it
Remarkable wines, pasta,
salads and fish.

**Antico Francischiello de Pep-
pino**, Via Partenope 27, Massa
Lubrense, tel: 081 533 9780,
www.francischiello.com
Crammed with local arts and
antiques, a veritable museum –
shaded terrace.

**Teatro Tasso**, Piazza S
Antonio, tel: 081 807 5525,
www.teatrotasso.com Regular
performances of *The Sorrento
Musical* in a dinner theatre.

*Outside Sorrento*

**Ristorante Don Alfonso**, Corso
Sant'Agata 11–13, Sant'Agata
sui due Golfi, tel: 081 878
0026, www.donalfonso.com
Renowned as one of the best
in Italy, service and style are
impeccable. A meal here is a
truly grand occasion.

**Restaurant Antica Osteria
Nonna Rosa**, 4 Privata Bonea
Road, Vico Equense, tel: 081
879 9055, www.osterianonna
rosa.it An early 18th-century
mansion now converted to a
Michelin-starred restaurant
presided over by chef Peppe
Guide. Cynical reviewers fall
over themselves to use words
like 'sublime', 'dazzling' and
'perfection', so he must be
doing something right!

## CLUBS AND BARS

**Bar Primavera**, Via Fuorimuro
20/Corso, Italia 142, tel:

081 878 3375 or 807 3252.
**Circolo dei Forestieri**
(Foreigners' Club), Via L. De
Maio 35, tel: 081 877 3263.
**Blu Blu**, Internet Café, Via
Fuorimura 20/D, tel: 081
807 4854.

## SHOPPING

Numerous small shops in the
town selling luxury items,
specializing in clothes, leather,
linens, shoes, pottery and local
handicrafts. Shop owners
almost always speak English.

## TOURS AND EXCURSIONS

**Syrenbus** (tel: 081 807 4220,
www.syrenbus.com), a limousine service offering transfers.
Full and half day sightseeing.
The rail service offers lovely
views, too.

**Boat/Yacht Charter:** It is also
possible to charter private boats
for exploring the islands. Ask
the tourist office for a list of
local operators.

## USEFUL CONTACTS

*Tourist Offices*
*Sorrento*
Via L. De Maio 35, tel: 081
807 4033, www.sorrento
tourism.com
**Guide Centre**, Via degli Aranci
187, Sorrento, tel: 081 878
3061, or 877 2197,
www.guidecentre.com
**Vico Equense**, Via San Ciro 16,
tel: 081 879 8826, or 801
6146, www.vicoturismo.it
**Castellammare di Stabia**,
Piazza Matteotti 34,
tel: 081 871 1334,
www.stabiatourism.it

# 7
# The Amalfi Drive

This is undoubtedly one of the most famous of all scenes, the Costa Amalfitana (Amalfi Coast). Get ready for a treat and a slow drive; speeding is definitely not recommended. Try to avoid weekends too, for many local people are doing the drive themselves then. This relatively short 80km (50-mile) stretch of strand is claimed to be the most beautiful coast in Italy. The impressive corniche style road ripples and turns, flips up and down as it hugs the shore southwest from Salerno, along coves, cliffs, beaches, groves and rocky inland heights all the way along the south coast of the Sorrentine peninsula. It constantly surprises. There is a kaleidoscope of changing views of land and sea. Revealed is a wildly varied and lush landscape against a serene drop of contrasting blues, the sea and the sky. It also shines with a necklace of historic towns.

These ancient little settlements use their very limited space, often a sheer cliff drop to the sea, with incredible ingenuity. You will be surprised at the way tiny towns can pack themselves into these tight steep spaces, offering room along its narrow, often stepped, streets only for the foot walker and maybe barrows, bikes and carts. Below are the always necessary fishing harbours, complete with beached or bobbing boats. You will also get a glimpse of Saracen watch towers, tiny churches, white and colour washed houses, rampant with pretty flowers standing along layers of narrow terraces. There are also beautiful gardens filled with vegetables, and backed with vines, olive, almond and lemon trees.

### Don't Miss

**\*\*\* The Amalfi Coast:** one of the world's loveliest stretches of coast, with natural scenery and local architecture.
**\*\*\* Amalfi:** offers charm and history in a ravishing setting.
**\*\*\* Ravello:** a complete hill town with two lovely gardens.
**\*\* Positano:** a little resort town in a dramatic setting – cliffs and whitewashed houses overlooking the sea.
**\* The Grotta dello Smeraldo:** the Emerald Grotto with similar reflected lighting effects to the Blue Grotto on Capri, but brilliant green.

**Opposite:** *The charming town of Positano descends the cliff in steep steps.*

**Below:** *The lush gardens in the Villa Rufolo in Ravello, are a profusion of colour, and present panoramic views.*

## RAVELLO

The entry point to the drive is the town of Salerno, reached from the A3 toll road to Pompeii and Naples. Turn at the sign for Vietri sul Mari for the S163, the beginning of the Amalfi Drive in the direction of Ravello. Consider hiring a car for the day to allow you the freedom to stop in parking places and admire the stunning views along the road (some roads are one-way).

For the kind of visitor who adores Italian charm, the village of Ravello is perfect, an Italian gem in a lovely setting. This scattering of houses along a hill, surrounded by low mountains, which at a colder time of year can be snow swept, presents a lovely prospect from a distance. As so many visitors have found, this is a superlatively lovely place. High on its hilltop over 305m (1000ft) up, it surveys the world, all the way down to Amalfi and the sea, an eagle's eyrie with ledges of gardens, hanging plants and dramatic viewpoints.

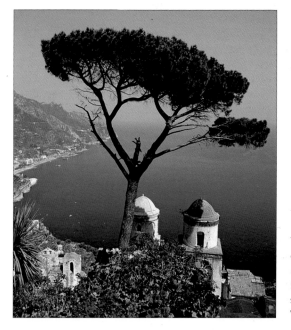

Opposite the cathedral, the Norman castle of the **Villa Rufolo** dates to the 11th century although much of it is 13th century in a peculiar mix of Saracen and Norman, only found in Italy. It was the home of the area's most powerful family, a palace for popes, also a king, its Gothic entry leading to a Moorish courtyard with elegant arches in interlaced Sicilian style. This former cloister is dominated with a formidable, if crumbling keep. Writer Boccaccio stayed here and even Wagner loosened his

Teutonic crown to be seduced by the beauties of Ravello – he liked it so much he made the garden into a magical setting, in his opera *Parsifal*. The famous gardens with their coastal views do indeed seem an enchanted place.

There is, however, a second Ravello garden that is even more impressive. A short distance from the central piazza, look for a stepped street leading to the twin churches of **San Francesco** (St Francis – pause to view the 13th-century cloister) and **Santa Chiara** (Church of St Clare). Beyond is the **Villa Cimbrone**. Here you find a witty exercise in gardening, opening to lawns and English rose beds, which rarely seem at home in such settings. This lovely garden with its odd cloister (look for the droll little images of the Seven Deadly Sins) and the nymph's grotto, contains a number of arbours, paths and statuary of varied origins. You are then seduced along to the final surprise as cool mossed walks with overhanging foliage end in a wide alley and a belvedere studded with marble busts that presents fabulous views of the hills and the Amalfi coast below.

Ravello's **cathedral** was started in 1086 and as so often happened in Italy, altered in the 18th century as new fashions dictated. Its façade testifies to this. Within, its ancient columns have been uncovered, cleaned and restored. Go inside, for the church is extraordinary for its rich and fantastic interior mosaics, mostly from the 13th century. The inlaid marble pulpit by Niccolo di Foggia is a remarkable and dramatic one; an

## ENGLISH GARDENER

It was in the late 19th century that **Lord Grimthorpe**, acquired and remodelled the Villa Cimbrone, and it is very much his creation. Here is yet another English aristocrat caught up with the romantic aspects of Italy, living away from home and busy employing his fortune in the creation of a legend. The two boars carved over the entrance make up the Grimthorpe Crest, and the garden's creator himself is buried nearby.

eagle soars above it and it is perched in Northern Italian Romanesque style on sculpted lions. In its mosaics the animals are lively, and equally splendid is a second smaller monument, an ambo with more mosaics of Jonah and the Whale, mostly in green. Look at the 12th-century bronze door, by Barisano da Trani. It has 54 sculpted panels of the life of Christ and his saints. In a side chapel the blood of the patron saint of the cathedral, San Pantaleone, is kept, and it is said to liquify miraculously every year. A small museum in the crypt contains additional mosaics and sculpture, including a silver reliquary head.

More antique columns line the little **church of St John**, which was also touched up in the 18th century but frescoes in the crypt and a grand early pulpit survive. There is a cameo shop with examples of cameos and coral. If you are robust and it isn't too hot you can try your legs on the climbing pathways, for most of the town is inaccessible to motorized transport.

A lovely time to walk around the town of covered passages, flights of steps and tiny alleys is the early morning, or the afternoon, when the upland air is warm and clear, and the views are at their best. Ravello's town centre is small and compact and there are several central hotels to stay at; stylish places with gardens and wide views, their rooms decorated with antiques. There are many possibilities for lunch or dinner on terraces, or in dining rooms – a chance to try the local wines too, so ask wine waiters for advice. They are not fine wines, but still well worth sampling, and you should certainly eat in good style.

If you are planning to stay for a few days, Ravello is an excellent choice for a centre of exploration being almost half way along the Amalfi Drive. You will find it an excellent town if you want to simply get away and relax in beautiful settings. In the hotter months the hilltop place is cooler too, and for day outings there are regular bus connections down to Amalfi. You descend from Ravello on a good winding road and cross the Dragon River Valley turning right to pass the village of Atrani and then heading for your next port of call, Amalfi.

## AMALFI

Amalfi claims a long and lively history that stretches back to the empire of Byzantium. Supposedly founded by Roman citizens who left Rome to escape invading barbarian hordes, the area began to recover early in the 9th century, and rapidly established itself as the chief town of the coast. With a burgeoning population, Amalfi grew into a leading city and by AD958 was the seat of a duke.

There is lots to do and see here. The 11th-century Duomo cannot be missed in its theatrical setting at the top of a flight of steps. It could be the opening scene of Cavalleria Rusticana in which the steps are crowded with chanting spectators at the start of the Easter ceremony. The **Duomo di Sant'Andrea** is on Piazza del Duomo. The church was remodelled in the 11th century and the glittering façade, which you approach up a flight of steps, was renovated in the 19th century. The only original part is the campanile with its multidomed top. Most interesting are the imposing bronze doors, cast in Constantinople in 1065, following a fashion of these parts for massive portals. (The mosaics are much later, but based on the Sicilian-Byzantine original.) If you like Baroque, the interior with its ceiling of wooden inlay will definitely appeal.

It's worth searching out the lovely 13th-century **Cloister of Paradise**, with its double columns and a set of interesting sarcophagi. Only open at certain hours, the Chiostro del Paradiso combines austerity with Arab decoration. In the crypt are kept relics of the cathedral's patron apostle, St Andrew, filched from Constantinople during the

### SIGHTSEEING IN STYLE

Although much of the area around Naples is well served by train and bus services, the **Amalfi Drive** itself is less fortunate. It is nicest if you are driven along this road, for even though it is so scenically notable it is also necessary to maintain constant control as it is **narrow**, **twisting** and **cliff hugging**. A driver will really not be able to enjoy it properly so consider asking the hotel to send a car for you. They usually will, though it is not a cheap option.

**Below:** *Lying between cliff and sea, Amalfi town is a splendid place to wander around. The churches and houses are situated above the colourful harbour.*

## PAPERMAKING

An ancient craft of fine **paper-making** is still practised here right in the town, and fine watermarked stationery or special paper for painting in watercolour is produced. Dating back to the 11th century, papermaking at the little factory and the paper-mill involves processing the handmade product all the way from pulp to paper.

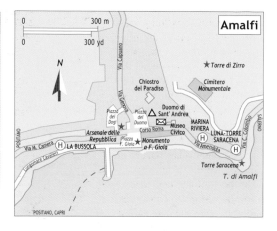

**Opposite:** *The Duomo di Sant'Andrea dominates the town's main piazza. As you walk up the many stairs, admire the façade, decorated in fine mosaics.*
**Below:** *The rocky coast of the Amalfi, overlooking the clear azure sea.*

Crusade of 1206. The cathedral also contains a museum of sculptures, pictures and gems.

In its early days of glory, Amalfi was a trading city like Italy's other maritime republics, Venice, Pisa and Genoa, supplying galleys for the Crusades and ply-ing for goods as far away as Constantinople and the Orient. Amalfi still retains links with the three other Italian maritime cities, now much bigger than this little

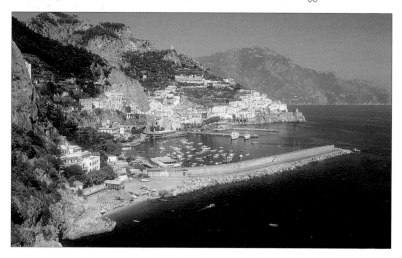

town, which has long been confined and prevented from sprawl by its restricted site. Amalfi was the first city in the world to codify maritime law and navigation. In the 11th century, the *Tavoli Amalfitane* was proclaimed, regulating all ships using the Mediterranean and establishing laws that were used until the 17th century. This book of maritime laws is now housed in the Town Hall. Amalfi was to become the first of Italy's Maritime Republics in AD840, then soon after it was made a dukedom, and ruled by a doge. Its affluence continued growing well past the 11th century. Amalfi's ships, made in the Republic's arsenal, rode far and wide over the inland sea, and it was crusaders from this tiny place who founded the Knights of St John.

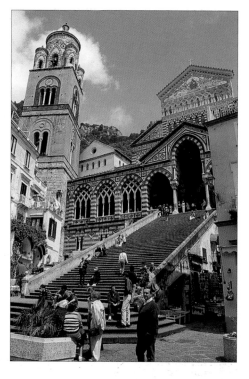

The ranks of white houses of Amalfi rear up against a brilliant sky as you approach the principal town of the coast, most notably from the edge of the sea. Its medieval sea trading brought great riches to the cliffside town which gave its name to the Amalfi Coast, and this opulent period is reflected today in its monuments and buildings. Now its port is reduced, but as an important and ever-popular resort, Amalfi offers many small attractions as well as major sights. The town has two main streets, **Via Capuano** and **Via Genova**, commencing at the cathedral's piazza. They are both lined with shops and cafés, galleries and studios. Balconies lean out over the streets, and striking up and down off the two streets are small passages worth exploring, as they very often lead to lovely, tiny

## MARITIME COMPETITION

Venice, Genoa, Pisa and Amalfi partake in an **annual regatta**. Although Amalfi is the smallest of the ancient maritime republics, and has a very limited harbour space, it still manages to hold the annual regatta, which alternates among the four. A set of special costumes is kept in the town hall just for this event. The duomo is dedicated to Saint Andrew, patron saint of sailors everywhere.

gardens and piazzas with fountains. Look for the **Piazza Flavio Gioia**, named for the local man who, supposedly, invented (or perhaps just perfected) the mariner's compass. He is certainly looking at a compass in the statue standing before the Town Hall.

In this ancient little city and its satellite towns, even the hotels are very special and often in the oldest and most surprising buildings, ranging from palaces to religious foundations. Though it has to be said facilities are completely modern even if the furnishings are often antique. The **Cappucino Convento** in Amalfi, now a grand hotel, sits on a high point reached by an elevator up the cliff. It's a lovely place to sit and admire the view from under grape arbours, or from the garden terraces. The **Luna Convent**, also a hotel at present, is original too – maybe St Francis wasn't as ascetic as history claims, for he certainly found a fine place to perch his establishment. Some 12th-century buildings remain, a cloister too, all adding to the charm of this hotel within a Saracen tower and a medieval monastery. A short walk up from the cathedral, it is still owned and managed by the same family – they have been here since 1825 – and it is certainly the oldest hotel in town. There is a swimming pool, gardens, and sea views. The owners are very proud of the fact that the peripatetic Henrik Ibsen wrote one of his masterpieces, *A Doll's House*, here.

## INSIDE AN EMERALD

The strange Grotta dello Smeraldo, not far from Amalfi, is a flooded sea cavern infused with eerie reflected light of a brilliant emerald green. The cavern floor has been altered due to earth movements and there are underwater stalactites and a bizarre submerged crib. The Smeraldo Grotto is accessible by an elevator, or stairs down from the road or by sea.

## POSITANO

Positano was part of the Amalfi Republic in the 9th–11th centuries; and again in the 16th–17th centuries, when it was a trading centre which actually rivalled bigger maritime cities in Italy. Positano has always been popular as a resort, in spite of its extraordinary terrain. It has a virtually vertical aspect, for the little town tumbles in terraces, paths, passages and flights of steps down a steep slope towards the sea. Take special care on wet days. The town itself is alluring, with fishermen's dwellings piled alongside grand villas above a small sandy beach lined with painted fishing boats. You would not think there was a possibility of tucking in another place to eat or stay in such a vertically inclined settlement. Yet there has been further controlled development of this picturesque town of small whitewashed houses with a Moorish look. It now has a permanent population of about 4000. One road

### WINTER FESTIVITIES

If you want to see the coast in an unusual and dramatic light, come at **Christmas** or **New Year**. The weather is usually mild, and there are fireworks and street entertainers. Special dishes of the season, such as game, wild boar, and codfish, appear on menus.

**Opposite:** *The narrow streets in Amalfi are lined with appealing boutiques.*
**Below:** *Positano ends at the sea with the Marina Grande pebble beach, marked with fishing boats.*

## SIREN SONG

Off in the sea to the south-west of Positano are the tiny islands known as **Li Galli**. According to legend, these were the islands where **Sirens** supposedly perched, singing their alluring notes to passing sailors to strand Odysseus on the rocks. Certainly the islands, if not the Sirens themselves, attracted Rudolf Nureyev who lived here when visiting the Amalfi coast.

gives vehicular access and, believe it or not, there is a small bus that runs around, though many hotels and apartments have only pedestrian access.

Positano town is special in a direct way, it remains essentially a fishermen's village in spite of the sophist-icated visitors who flock here from all over the world, all year round. It retains a sweet compelling charm, pastel-pretty by day and romantic at night with its alluring restaurants under the stars. There really is very little to offer those in search of antiquities or splendid architecture. You might say it just has itself to parade, and that for many is enough when they come to visit this pretty little town, ranged along its ledges and ter-races down the sea facing cliff. There is a small and lively harbour, a cathedral and lots of little shops, as well as plenty of places to eat and drink. As a place to stay it is unique, however, with its enormous charm

**Right:** *Positano's Moorish-style architecture.*

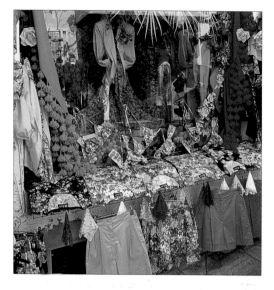

**Left:** *One of the stalls in Positano, displaying the colourful beachwear for which the town is famous.*

and lovely setting of cliff and cove, and inlet. The gardens are as grand as anywhere else on this magical coast, the streets are very steep and often stepped. What Positano does have, is a huge range of places to stay; from the grand to the simple, from the most expensive to the reasonable, and some of them are quite special and beloved by their regular guests. There is the eccentric San Pietro, there are converted villas (the Bucca di Bacco and the Poseidon) and even a one-time palace, the Palazzo Murat, once lived in by Napoleon's brother-in-law, the king of Naples. Believe it or not, there are actually 72 hotels here. Finding staff must be difficult indeed.

## SMALLER RESORTS

Do not feel restricted to stay at one of the larger settlements along the drive, for there are many small resorts to choose from along a coast whose biggest attraction is the splendid **Grotta dello Smeraldo** (Emerald Cave). Visit **Conca dei Marini** with its ruined watch tower, **Marina di Praia,** a small beach surrounded by fisher-

### STAR TURNS

Many great artists have lived or worked on this coast. **Boccaccio** made it a setting for a scene in the Decameron (1349–53). In Positano the great Russian maestro, **Sergei Diaghilev,** worked with the Ballets Russes that took Paris and London by storm in the first decades of the 20th century. In his entourage were **Nijinsky**, **Picasso**, **Massine** and **Stravinsky**. **Franco Zeffirelli** is the latest international star to claim a toehold here.

**Above:** *The pastel and white houses and shops are closely packed together in the quiet town of Atrani.*

men's houses, or **Vettica Minore**. If you want a quiet beach resort for a perch, **Praiano** is an ideal little place. Very quiet, yet close to Positano, it offers a choice of accommodation, and has a picturesque little harbour and a really good beach. For those in search of nightly entertainment there is a disco beside the beach here. At any of the small ports or resorts, there will be good restaurants usually with alfresco terraces and the food is generally delicious, especially the frutta di mare, or crustacea, and pasta with fish.

Easily missed, although just off the main road as you drive to Amalfi, the little fishing port of **Atrani** is well worth a visit. From the piazza explore the narrow stepped streets rising up the steep hill past tiny courtyards and tall white houses, until you find several little restaurants at the top of the town for a welcome pause or a meal. In the town are two notable churches, one, San Salvatore, has a bronze door similar in style to Amalfi's.

Although the route to the mainland from Amalfi is still fascinating, with the vivid sea beside you, and lots of scenic surprises, it is a less exclusive area. Consequently on the road to Salerno there are interesting, less visited small resorts. These can be well worth a stop off. Not far from Atrani, and on the sea with a small sand beach, is Minori. It's a charming village with a surprise – an ancient site, a 1st-century Roman villa, which can be visited. There are hotels and restaurants in the close-packed streets behind the shady seafront drive. There's a tourist office, too.

If most of the seaside settlements are too quiet and you want a more lively place, try Maiori, a very different sort of resort a little further on. Here there are lots of busy bars and surprisingly good eating places for fish along a long, wide beach. A nice walk, or a local bus takes you on to a real discovery – tiny Cetara.

## VIETRI SUL MARE

A small town at the very beginning of the route, that is not so concerned with lazing by the sea and sunbathing even though it is right on the coast, is Vietri sul Mare near Salerno, at the turn of the major A3 road. This little place with its terraced houses climbing up the slopes of the hills, is devoted to just one thing – the making of fine ceramics. A good place to consider for a visit if the weather turns cloudy or damp – which it can do, even here. In Vietri, you can stroll at a slow pace, from place to place, to compare what is on offer from whole dinner services to solo items, or choose from the many outside stands, which seem to crowd every street. There are several factories, and quite small workshops too, so there is a great deal of choice and a lot to consider before you part with your pennies. It is a good idea to check at the Tourist Office, which is located on Vietri's central piazza, before you wander as they will have information on special exhibitions, master craftsmen and how to visit smaller studios and artists at work. Vietri itself also offers splendid views of the coast, and you can easily combine a day out here with a trip into Salerno, its bigger neighbour.

## CETARA

If you prefer a dip in a clear sea from a tiny beach, try Cetara. This fishing village, pressed into its narrow valley, only has one hotel, called the Cerus, with its own private beach.

### WELL CONNECTED

Main transport connections can be made from near Vietri, for it is an exit off the A3 autoroute, as is Salerno. This city is connected to the main rail system so you can get fast trains here for Naples, or further on to Rome and the North. In Naples the daily paper lists train and boat departures for the whole area.

## Amalfi Coast at a Glance

The Amalfi Coast has similar weather and temperature conditions to Capri and the islands. Note, however, that the drive itself can become very busy on weekends and during public holidays.

Superb views from your **car** as you follow the famous Amalfi Drive, or you can take sea connections by **ferry** from other resorts, or Naples. Some visitors even take **helicopters** – if you are staying at the San Pietro in Positano!

### Amalfi and the Amalfi Coast
*LUXURY*
**Grand Hotel Convento di Amalfi**, Via Annunziatella 46, tel: 089 873 6711, www.nh-hotels.com Very grand old style at this 12th-century convent with wonderful views and a cliff-top terrace. Take the lift up from the main road to this marvellous place. Now a hotel with 53 bedrooms, many have balconies and sea views, antique furnishings and fine décor. Take a stroll before dinner in the terraced gardens.
**Luna-Torre Saracena**, Via P Comite 33, tel: 089 871 002, www.hotellunaamalfi.com St Francis suposedly founded this monastery, now an 81-room hotel with views down to the sea. Some of the original 12th-century work and a cloister can still be seen. The hotel is enclosed within the old monastery and there's a Saracen tower, too. The same family have owned it since 1825 – it's Amalfi's oldest. It has lovely gardens and a pool.
**Santa Caterina**, Strada Statale Amalfitana 9, tel: 089 871 012, www.hotelsantacaterina.it Art Déco is becoming more and more fashionable, and this 99-room seaside hotel reflects the 20s style. It is the best place to stay in Amalfi. There is a sea-water pool, but you can also take a lift down to the beach. The hotel offers gardens, fine views, a terrace and even a gym. About 1km (0.5 mile) from Amalfi, along the coast road. There are separate villas.

*MID-RANGE*
**La Bussola**, Lungomare dei Cavalieri 1, tel: 089 871 533, www.labussolahotel.it A bit plain yet perfectly comfortable. This old converted mill is family run and has a terrace with good sea views.

*BUDGET*
**Lido Mare**, Largo Ducci Piccolomene 9, tel: 089 871 332, www.lidomare.it This hotel has a decided Moorish air, with whitewashed walls and arches in North African style. Cool and pleasing; some rooms have sea views.

### Positano
*LUXURY*
**San Pietro**, Via Laurito 2, tel: 089 875 455, www.ilsan pietro.it This very expensive modern hotel is almost hidden in a cliff-side, 1 mile east of Positano. High profile guests, from Princess Diana to film stars, have enjoyed its views and fine food. There's a pool, tennis courts and terraces, a helipad and a private beach.
**Palazzo Murat**, Via dei Mulini 23, Positano, tel: 089 875 177, www.palazzomurat.it This is a great little hotel (38 rooms) for those with a taste for history. Napoleon married off his relations to the aristocracy and Princess Murat was his sister. Stay in her palace – now a smart in-town hotel, yet not too expensive, with a court-yard garden. Closed in winter.

*MID-RANGE*
**Albergo Casa Albertina**, Via della Tavolozza 3, tel: 089 875 143, www.casalbertina.it A rooftop seafood restaurant adds to the appeal of this small and friendly 39-room hotel. In the centre of town, and with views down to the sea. Local crafts on display.
**Miramare**, Via Trara Genoino 25–27, tel: 089 875 002/3, www.miramarepositano.it Many people prefer this nice little hotel with lots of atmosphere to the large and grand. It has 29 rooms, 15 of which have great bathrooms, and the location is dramatic – on a cliff edge above the sea. Wide, perfect views from its terraces.
**La Buca di Bacco**, Via Rampa Teglia 8, tel: 089 875 699, www.bucadibacco.it Historic beachfront hotel with famous waterfront bar and restaurant

offering great Mediterranean and Neapolitan cuisine. The name comes from Bacchus, the jovial god of good drinking.

### BUDGET
**Maria Luisa**, Via Fornillo 42, tel/fax: 089 875 023, www.pensionemarialuisa.com A low priced and simple 10-room spot. Very friendly.

**Hotel Pasitea**, Via Pasitea 207, Positano, tel: 089 875 500, www.hotelpasitea.it B&B and bar, cool blue and white décor, fine cliff views, comfort, friendly service and a good position halfway up the cliff make this Best Western a good bet. Open all year.

### Ravello
#### LUXURY
**Palumbo**, Via San Giovanni del Toro 16, tel: 089 857 244, www.hotelpalumbo.it An old Moorish mansion with panoramic views. The Palazzo Confalone, is the setting for this very grandly designed and beautifully decorated hotel. You will be well catered for here. It is expensive, but there is also a cheaper modern annexe.

#### MID-RANGE
**Villa Maria**, Via Santa Chiara 2, tel: 089 857 255, www.villamaria.it There are two hotels here. The older Villa is next to the modern Giordano, both managed by the same family. Pool, terrace with gardens, 45 rooms, and not far from the centre of town.

#### BUDGET
**Villa Amore**, Via dei Fusco, tel/fax: 089 857 135, www.villaamore.it A 22-room converted villa with gardens and views from its high cliff perch. Nice location near town.

### WHERE TO EAT
#### Amalfi
**La Caravella**, Via Matteo Camera 12, tel: 089 871 029, www.ristorantelacaravella.it Local seafood is the speciality, as well as superb desserts. Medium-priced, rather plain in looks, but well worth a visit, though you should book ahead. Closed all Nov.

**Trattoria Da Gemma**, Via Frà Gerardo Sasso 9, tel: 089 871 345, www.trattoriadagemma.com An old-established, well-loved local restaurant. There is an open-air terrace and delicious local seafood. It is popular, so try to book in advance. Closed Aug.

#### Positano
**Chez Black**, Via Brigantino 19, tel: 089 875 036, www.chezblack.it Good pasta and pizza here, beside the harbour and beach. Try the seafood pasta and finish your meal with one of their excellent ice creams. Closed during the winter season.

**Ristorante-Pizzeria da Constantino**, Via Monte-pertuso 107, tel: 089 875 738, www.daconstantino.it High up at the back of the town, this is a delightfully friendly neighbourhood

restaurant, with a warm welcome, great unpretentious food and superb views. Open all year.

**Trattoria La Tagliata**, Via Tagliata 22, tel: 089 875 872, www.latagliata.com Dizzyingly high up the cliff, this family-run restaurant serves superb food, with all comers eating the same multi-course menu. Vegetarians give advance warning. Fri - Sun evenings only in winter.

#### Ravello
**Cumpà Cosimo**, Via Roma 44–46, tel: 089 857 156. Centrally located, and often crowded trattoria. Big servings. The accent is on their fine pasta dishes.

### SHOPPING
Lots of small places in town have a range of souvenirs (look for local handiwork and crafts), plus luxury goods of all kinds. For a few foreign language newspapers, or books try:

**Savo Bonaventura**, Via Repubbliche Marinare 17, Amalfi, tel: 089 871 180.

### USEFUL CONTACTS
#### Tourist Offices
**Positano**
Via Saraceno 1, tel: 089 875 067 or 875 760.
**Amalfi**
Corso Roma 19/21, tel: 089 871 107 or 872 619.
**Ravello**
Piazza Duomo 10, tel: 089 857 096 or 857 657.

# 8
# Salerno and Paestum

It is easy to overlook the coast and country running southeast of the Amalfi Drive. Yet it has many attractions and historic associations. Beaches and seascapes do predominate, yet there is much to discover inland and once embarked you may want to stay for a time, recognizing that the splendours of the Bay of Naples rather overshadow these simpler attractions. For the adventurous visitor, stretching along the Gulf of Salerno is a fascinating drive past villages and wide views to the important ancient sites of Paestum and Velia. Further to the south you will find the towns of Agropoli, Pioppi and Padula on longer excursions. From here the road goes on to the neighbouring province of Basilicata.

One of the cities here is a famous one, found 250 years ago and one of the most important discoveries in Italy. It is the large archeological site known as Paestum with its temples and museum. The modern town offers a wide beach shaded by pine woods. After a long drive down you find Padula, with its amazing monastery.

## SALERNO

The first town on the drive south is Salerno. The main road runs right down the front of the town along the shore hugging Lungomare Trieste with its green borders and palm trees. This is an active industrial port and naval centre, yet still offers much charm, and the extensive views over the Gulf of Salerno from here are very fine.

The town expands to the hillside behind. There is a castle on its hill above the Gulf and the old part of

---

## DON'T MISS

**★★★ Paestum:** one of the grandest temples in the world, set in a large archaeological site that was lost for centuries.
**★★ St Matthew, Duomo Salerno:** although much altered, the Romanesque cathedral has some remarkable features, from huge doors to inlaid pulpits and treasures in its museum.

---

**Opposite:** *Temple of Neptune, Paestum.*

Salerno

town stretches below it. Salerno is a busy port and centre for light industries, while small farms and market gardens surround it.

Once a more important city than Naples, the history of Salerno is a long complicated one going back to the Etruscans who founded it. Then came Rome, and after attaining considerable status more than 2000 years ago, Salerno became even more important as the capital city of later invaders from the north – the Lombards made it a principality. Around 1077 the Normans under Robert Guiscard founded the cathedral and the town prospered. It declined later and as a result Naples became the most important centre of the region.

On the 9th of September 1943 Salerno witnessed the invasion of the Allies who were to precipitate Italy's defeat in World War II. American soldiers of the 5th US Army landed south of the town and began the push up the peninsula as part of the offensive that eventually toppled the dictator Mussolini. The area saw much military action as the movement north to Rome began.

Although an important town and capital of its province, Salerno is often bypassed, which is a pity. Within its heart are several interesting sights, notably an extensive medieval section and the charming Via Mercanti with old shops and houses, one end focused on a very ancient monument, the Arco di Arechi, at its western limit, dating from the Lombard period.

The duomo, the Norman cathedral of St Matthew, has been much changed in the 900 years of its life, yet still retains some spectacular aspects, notably the great 12th-century bronze doors. These were made in

## CITY OF SOCRATES

Salerno gained this sobriquet connecting it with the great Greek philosopher when it was at its apogee and had become rich from trading. Its university was soon to be renowned and was well known among the foremost minds of the age, as scholars arrived to work and teach here. Particularly noted for its School of Medicine, it grew quickly under the Normans. Founded in the 11th century its international fame declined after the 13th.

Constantinople and of the same date are pulpits, inlaid with mosaics, in similar style to others in Campania. There is a museum attached, with relics, also a provincial museum with some fascinating finds from local archaeological digs.

## VELIA

Unlike its neighbour, Paestum, little remains of this city in the province of Cilento. It was an important centre, however, and there are extensive ruins. It was founded in 535BC by Greeks escaping the Persian advance, and soon became a prosperous port, later notable for its school of philosophy. Here Zeno became the originator of the Stoic philosophy and later succeeded his master Parmenides, one of the best known philosophers before Socrates. Once a base for Brutus after the death of Julius Caesar, Velia declined with the fading of Rome.

## PADULA

The impressive Certosa di Padula is a vast Carthusian monastery. It was built over several periods, much of it boldly tiled. There is a huge cloister (with fine views of the nearby hill town), elegant architecture, many

### DEADLY PESTS

Until its origins were known, and draining wetlands became an answer, malaria was a terrible scourge of Italy's low-lying marshy districts, from Tuscany to the toe of the boot. It was a major problem here at Paestum, lying near flat soggy fields, haunted by clouds of invading mosquitoes. Carrying the dreaded disease, the ensuing infections eventually decimated the inhabitants so much that even during the Roman Empire the people left. A long process had begun during which the town began slowly to fade away and die.

**Below:** *Salerno town and marina.*

**Right:** *About 40km (25 miles) from Salerno lie the ancient Greek ruins of Paestum, believed to have been founded around 600BC.*

chapels, secret gardens, shops and a surprising Spanish-style kitchen. A 5000-egg omelette was once made here! There's good accommodation at a nearby farm.

## PAESTUM

Paestum is an incredible place. This very important antique site was discovered in the mid-18th century during road building. The once great city of the coastal marshes lay hidden for many centuries, submerged under trees and bushes, now an open dry plain. Its outstanding temples are surprisingly well preserved today, standing in a sylvan setting of fields backed by hills. It was at first a Greek colony founded around 600BC, called Poseidonia. After a couple of centuries the city declined and was appropriated by Rome in 273BC. As a dwindling settlement Paestum lingered on into the medieval period, but subject to Saracen offensives and deadly malarial mosquitoes, it was eventually abandoned.

Now only a cluster of ancient gold and grey stone buildings with extensive fragments of fortifications, in its great days it must have been a magnificent city with miles of high walls surrounding temples, forum and houses. Here the splendidly simple Doric style is particularly well represented in pale yellow limestone, most notably in the magnificent Temple of Nettuno. Originally settled by Sybarites, who famously gave their name to standards of excessive luxury, the city reflects their elegance in the Tomb of the Diver, only discovered in 1968.

To walk around the ruins you will need plenty of time, so allow at least two hours. Follow the Via Sacra from the entry at the Porta della Giustizia. On the right you will see the Basilica dating from the town's very earliest days with its 50 unusually curved columns, and porch dedicated to Hera. Then there is the larger Temple of Neptune, also constructed of limestone, huge and best preserved of all. Next is the Forum with its portico and surrounding shops and just beyond the Ampitheatre (Roman) through which the modern road cuts, and finally the Gymnasium. The rovine, or ruins of ancient dwellings, cluster around these principal buildings and temples.

An unusual underground temple follows (Tempietto Sotteraneo), with a fine collection of bronze vases. The Temple of Ceres is next, dating from the 6th century BC. Originally built in honour of Athena it has columns, some pediments and a sacrificial altar. You can visit the Museum which contains Greek funerary murals which may be unique. They were contained within the Tomb of the Diver (Tuffatore), in which the diver is discovered in lively, lightly erotic frescoes. There are sculpted details from the temples here too, and handsome 6th-century BC low-relief metopes, notably featuring the feats of Hercules, from the sanctuary of Hera approximately 10km (6 miles) north of Paestum. (There are other elegant metopes on the site.)

You can stay at any one of many pleasant hotels in the modern settlement beside the beach, and there are nice restaurants, too, in this pleasant little seaside resort among pine trees.

**Paestum**

1. Basilica (Temple of Hera)
2. Temple of Neptune
3. Forum
4. Amphitheatre
5. Temple of Ceres
6. Underground Sacellum (Tempietto Sotteraneo)
7. National Museum
8. Piscina
9. Temple of Peace
10. Comitium
11. Macellum

Via Sacra

Porta della Giustizia

0        2000 m

0        2000 yd

N

# Salerno and Paestum at a Glance

Any time is good to visit, as like all of the coast, it has a **mild** and agreeable climate. Salerno has some tourist attractions but it is basically a business city with a lively port, much modernized after war damage in 1943 and rather scruffy. It's a useful place to find reasonable accommodation, however, for those who want a base for touring and don't want to spend a lot of money in the smart centres. Paestum does have a busy tourist visiting period from late **spring** to **autumn** with crowded times likely in Jul and Aug, when the great temples are popular with all sorts of tour groups. If you can, go out of season and you will see more.

This city is connected to the main rail system so you can get fast **trains** here for Naples, or further on to Rome and the North. There are plenty of trains from Naples to Salerno, and a regular train service from Salerno to Paestum. The station is at the Piazza Vittorio Veneto with local and city bus stops. **Bus** services go to Naples, Amalfi and Positano, from 119 Corso Garibaldi, the SITA station. Buses for Paestum and places further south leave Piazza della Concordia at the quayside. Paestum has organized tours. **Ferry** and **hydrofoil** services go to Amalfi and Positano, almost every hour from the harbour. For up-to-date timetables, check the local

newspapers. In Naples, the daily paper lists train and boat departures for the whole area. If travelling by car, Salerno is easily reached, as main connections to and from the A3 autoroute can be made for Salerno and also Vietri. There are well-marked exit signs.

Salerno is very much a business city and tourists are not often seen here. Accommodation and dining are geared to it's importance as a port and naval installation, so you will find that the hotels are rather modern and businesslike too.

### Salerno
#### LUXURY
**Grand Hotel**, via Lungomare Clemente Tafuri 1, tel: 089 704 1111, www.grandhotel salerno.com Chic and sleek and modern, all angular and white, with sharp corners, the Grand lounges on the Salerno seafront like a beached cruise ship. It also has the facilities: the spa, the pool, the restaurants, the bar and the prices.

#### MID-RANGE
**Plaza Hotel**, Vittorio Veneto 42, tel: 089 224 477, plaza@ general.it www.plazasalerno.it Central, this air-conditioned, 44-room hotel, is clean and simple. There is a bar, but unfortunately no dining room. The parking lot at the back of the hotel is a real advantage as the streets can get quite busy in the summer.

**Villa Rizzo Resort & Spa**, Via Gerardo Napolitano, San Cipriano Picentino, tel: 089 862 108, www.villarizzo.com A gorgeous setting overlooking peach groves in the hills near Salerno, 10 antique-decorated rooms, a family welcome, large pool, spa and delicious home-cooked food. Wonderful.

**Hotel Fiorenza**, Via Trento 145, Salerno, tel: 089 338 800, www.hotelfiorenza.it Cool, clean colours, sea views, a friendly welcome and convenient location on the Salerno seafront combine with very reasonable prices to make this a popular choice amongst those who prefer to stay outside Naples.

#### BUDGET
**Youth Hostel**, Via Luigi Guercio 112, tel: 089 790 251. **Hotel K**, Lungomare Colombo, Via D. Somma 47, tel: 089 752 720, www.hotelk.it Comfortable waterfront boutique hotel with a roof garden, snack bar and bar.

### Paestum
There are hotels in nearby towns, and several simple pensiones and camping sites along the coast close to the site, though some only offer stopovers with meals. If you want to stay in Paestum and enjoy the sandy and rarely crowded beach, check the tourist information office for suggestions. (located close to the Paestum site entrance).

## Salerno and Paestum at a Glance

*MID-RANGE*

**Mec Paestum**, at Licinela, Via Tiziano 23, tel: 0828 722 444, www.hotelmec.com Has 52 air-conditioned rooms and suites, with a lovely garden, pool, a tennis court, private beach and a restaurant. There is also access for the disabled.
**Best Western Hotel Esplanade**, Via Poseidonia, Paestum, tel: 0828 851 043, www.hotel esplanade.com Modern, touristy, but comfortable, with gardens, a pool, beach frontage, good food and near the ruins.

*Alternative Accommodation*
**Azienda Agrituristica Seliano**, Tenuta Seliano, Paestum, tel: 0828 723 634, www.agri turismoseliano.it An unusual find, a farm in the local countryside mainly producing milk from buffalos to make mozzarella. This farmhouse is for longer stays with meals offered, there is also a swimming pool and a lovely garden. At Capaccio, 14km (9 miles) from Paestum, the Aziendo Agricola scheme also has riding stables.
**Domus Laeta**, via Flavio Gioia, Giungano (Sa), tel: 0828 880 177, www.domuslaeta.com Fabulous agriturismo in historic building (c. 1600) with mountain, sea and temple views, antique-filled rooms, pool, and delicious home-cooked food. Mid-range.

*Padula*
**Agriturismo Aia Antica**, Via Fusara 4, Padula, tel: 0975 74550, www.agriturismo

aiantica.it Farm holidays, full board, modern accommodation, local food served.

### WHERE TO EAT

Again not a notable town for food, but plenty of small satisfactory restaurants along the main roads and nice little family places too, as well as the inevitable chain snackeries. For those who are self catering, there are many food shops and a market too. Amongst the better restaurants in Salerno are the **Vicolo della Neve** (Vicolo della Neve 24) and the **Hosteria Canali** (Via Canali 34). Otherwise there are several other cheaper places to eat. Shop locally and go to the beach or the nearby woods for an enjoyable picnic. *See* Cilento, below.

### SHOPPING

Salerno has some surprisingly good small shops situated along the busy Corso V. Emanuele, which leads to the ancient town centre, with yet more smaller shops. It is very busy on weekends. Don't waste time and money on cheap stalls by the entrance to sites. Off-site souvenir stalls can be very mediocre. Postcards can be alright though. Some Italian sites do have their own approved shops with excellent items, however. Otherwise it is better to wait and check the shops and art galleries in major towns where the quality should be much better.

### CILENTO

An unusual spot for lovers of the countryside is the Cilento, an area that extends into the sea just south of Paestum, and runs all the way to the neighbouring province of Basilicata to the south. A mountainous and wild place, it offers all sorts of possibilities for nature lovers' exploration – bird-watching, and tracks for hiking, running and riding. On the whole it is a beautiful and unspoiled part of the country, especially inland, where there is a natural forest of ancient olive trees and chestnuts. The Cilento has a coastal area with reasonable hotels, especially for a short stay. Small resorts along the beach edge are worth exploring for good value rooms and food.

### TOURS AND EXCURSIONS

Paestum is not far from Salerno, closer to Agripoli in the south. Paestum is one of the most popular of the historic sites of Campania with Europe's finest Doric temples. There are plenty of possibilities for tours, mostly with guides. When visiting, allow for a whole day as there is lots to see here. Ask for details at tourist offices.

### USEFUL CONTACTS

*Tourist Offices*
*Salerno*
Train Station, Piazza Vittorio Veneto, tel: 089 231 432.
*Paestum*
On the main road, at the entrance to the archaeological site, tel 0828 811 016.

# Travel Tips

## Tourist Information
### Italian Tourist Offices
www.italiantourism.com
**Australia**, Level 4, 46 Market Street, Sydney, NSW 2000, tel: 02 926 21666, e-mail: sydney@enit.it
**Canada**, 175 Bloor Street E, Suite 907 South Tower, Toronto M4W 3R8, tel: 00 1 416 925 4882, e-mail: toronto@enit.it
**UK**, 1 Princes St, London W1B 2AY, tel: 020 7408 1254, e-mail: london@enit.it
**USA**, 630 Fifth Ave, Ste 1565, New York 10111, NY, tel: 00 1 212 245 5618, e-mail: newyork@enit.it Also offices in Los Angeles and Chicago. Another useful website for information on Naples is www.seenaplesea.it

### Embassies and Consulates
**Australia**, 12 Grey Street, Deakin, Canberra A C T 2600, tel: 06 273 3333, fax: 06 273 4223, e-mail: ambasciata.canberra@esteri.it
**Canada**, 275, Slater Street, 21st floor, Ottawa, Ontario K1P 5H9, tel: 613 232 2401/2/3, fax: 613 233 1484, e-mail: ambasciata.ottawa @esteri.it
**New Zealand**, 34 Grant Road, Wellington, tel: 04 473 5339 or 472 9302, fax: 04 472 7255, e-mail: ambasciata. wellington@esteri.it

**South Africa**, 796 George Avenue, Arcadia, Pretoria, tel: 012 423 0000, fax: 012 435 547, e-mail: segreteria.pretoria@esteri.it
**UK**, 14 Three Kings Yard, London W1K 4EH, tel: 020 7312 2200, fax: 020 7312 2230, e-mail: ambasciata. londra@esteri.it
Consulate, 38 Eaton Place London SW1X 8AN, tel: 020 7235 9371. Consulates also in **Edinburgh** and **Manchester**.
**USA**, Consulate-General, 690, Park Avenue, New York, NY 10065, tel: 00 1 212 737 9100, e-mail: info.newyork@ esteri.it The embassy is in Washington DC, with other consulates in Boston, Detroit, Chicago, Philadelphia, Los Angeles, Houston, Miami, Newark, San Francisco, with many sub-offices.

### Foreign Consulates in Naples
**South Africa**, Via Stendhal 23, tel: 081 552 5835; **UK**, Via dei Mille 40, tel: 081 423 8911; **USA**, Piazza della Repubblica, tel: 081 583 8111.

## Entry Requirements
EU citizens need a national ID card; all other visitors require a valid passport. Visas are not required by any citizens of the Commonwealth or the USA for stays of up to three months. Other nationalities should

check with the nearest embassy or consulate before travelling.

## Customs and Entry Regulations
Italy is part of the European Union and standard EU customs allowances apply. Guidelines for goods bought duty-paid within the EU are 800 cigarettes, 400 cigarillos, 200 cigars, 10 litres of spirits, 20 litres of fortified wine, 90 litres of wine and 110 litres of beer. For duty-free or goods bought outside the EU, allowances are: 200 cigarettes or 100 cigarillos or 50 cigars or 250g tobacco; 1 litre of spirits or 2 litres of sparkling or fortified wine and 2 litres of still wine; 50g perfume or 250cc of toilet water.

## Health
Italy is a healthy destination, with good food, clean water, few serious diseases, and excellent medical care. There is no need to have any in-oculations. The water is safe, although mineral water is freely available. In high sum-mer, take sunblock, a hat and drink plenty of fluids to counter the intense heat. There are reciprocal arrangements with all other EU countries and with Australia. UK citizens should apply for a European Health

Insurance Card (EHIC) from a post office or online at www.ehic.org.uk If taken ill, ask at a pharmacy (identified by a green cross), as they are able to help with many minor ailments and prescribe a wide variety of medicines. Each town operates a rota for late night and weekend opening.
**Farmacia Almasalus**, Piazza Dante 71, tel: 081 549 9336, stays open 24 hours a day. If you need a doctor, ask your hotel, or check the yellow pages under Unità Sanitaria. If in doubt, call the **Guardia Medica**, tel: 081 563 1111.
**A&E departments (Pronto Soccorso)**, Ospedale Cardarelli, Via Cardarelli 9, tel: 081 747 2956; Ospedale dei Pellegrini, Via Portamedina 41, tel: 081 563 3234; and Ospedale San Paolo, Via Terracina 219; tel: 081 768 6284.
**Insurance:** It is advisable to take out comprehensive travel insurance to cover medical and other emergencies.

## Transport

**By Air:** From London, the easiest way to get to Naples is with easyjet (www.easyjet. com) who fly daily from Gatwick. The only other airline flying direct is British Airways (www.britishairways. com). There are also charter flights in season and international departures from other major cities across Europe.
**Naples Capodochino Airport** is about 7km (4 miles) from the city centre. There are no rail links, but there are excellent bus services into Piazza

Garibaldi (by the Central Station) and Piazza Municipio in the town centre every 20–30 mins. From Central Station, you can connect with the Circumvesuviana (see below) to Sorrento, the tram, metro or the main Trenitalia network and city bus network.
Flight information tel: 848 888 777 or +39 081 751 5471 (from mobiles or abroad). Lost luggage assistance tel: 199 280 180, www.naples-airport.com
**By Train:** There are excellent, frequent and remarkably affordable rail connections with the rest of Italy via Italian state railways,
**Trenitalia** (tel: 892 021, www.trenitalia.it), with services to Rome at least once an hour (journey time: 2–3 hours, dependent on the type of train). You pay more for faster services and must have advance reservations on the fastest EC (Eurocity) services. A smaller number of international services connect via Milan or Rome. Validate your ticket in the machine at the entrance to the platform before boarding. **Stazione Centrale**, Piazza Garibaldi, tel: 1478 88088 (numero verde; open 07:00–21:00), is Naples' main station. Many of the trains from Rome also stop at **Campi Flegrei** and **Mergellina** (recommended).
**Local trains:** There are local trains, the Circumvesuviana (tel: 800 053 939, www. vesuviana.it) and the Circumflegrea/Cumana which encircle the Bay of Naples to north and south, taking in many of the main tourist

sights including Pompeii, Herculaneum, and Sorrento in the south, and Pozzuoli and Cumae in the north. There are no trains on the Amalfi Coast (take a train to Sorrento or Salerno then take a bus); tel: 800 001 616, www.sepsa.it For Salerno and Caserta, use Trenitalia services.
**By ferry:** There are regular ferry services to Naples from Sicily, Sardinia and the Aeolian Islands, run by Tirrenia (tel: 892 123), Snav, TT Lines (tel: 081 575 2192) and Siremar (tel: 892 123). There is also a busy network of ferries between Naples, various towns around the bay and the islands, including Sorrento, Capri, Ischia, Procida, and Pozzuoli. Some services leave from Mergellina, but most leave from Beverello, at the foot of the Palazzo Reale in the city centre. The different operators all have separate ticket kiosks in front of the jetties and sorting out timetables can get confusing.

Operators include: SNAV (tel: 081 428 5555, www.snav.it); NLG (tel: 081 552 073, www.navlib.it), Neapolis (tel: 081 552 7209, www.caprinfo.it), Alilauro (tel: 081 497 2201, www.alilaurio.it), Caremar (tel: 081 551 3882, www.caremar.it), Medmar (tel: 081 333 4411, www.medmarnavi.it).

**Transport within the city:**
There is a growing network of metros, trams, buses and four funiculars, all of which take the same tickets; tel: 800 568 866, www.metro.na.it See also Naples At a Glance, p. 50.

**By Coach:** There are coach services to all other major cities in Italy, and even a few international routes, such as the London–Naples direct service by National Express Eurolines (UK, tel: 08717 818 181, www.eurolines.com). Coaches fan out to towns across the bay area, the Amalfi Coast, and southern Italy. Most leave from Piazza Garibaldi, Piazza Vittoria or Napoli Porto Immacolatella.

**By Car:** Italy's motorways are all toll roads, and can prove expensive, but credit card payments are accepted. Inner city driving in Naples is to be avoided at all costs, but there is a fast 20km (12-mile) ring road surrounding the city if you need to get past. Rural roads are well-built and reasonably empty; the exception is the Amalfi Drive which becomes one-way in summer to cope with the volume of traffic. EU drivers may use their national **license**; all others need an international driving permit. If you take your own car, from within an EU country, your own insurance policy should cover you; however, you should top it up to get comprehensive accident and breakdown cover as the costs of dealing with even minor problems can be multiplied many times over if abroad. Some national motoring organizations offer reciprocal arrangements with other countries so check before travelling. Keep all relevant papers, including the car's ownership documentation, in the car at all times. You may not need a car – public transport is excellent in the area. If you do, shop around, prices are high and very variable. To **hire a car** you must be at least 21 and have had a clean license for a full year. The cost of insuring your excess can be extremely high; Insurance4CarHire (www.insurance4carhire.com) offers a useful alternative via a cheap annual policy.

**Avis**, www.avis.co.uk Offices at the airport, Central Station and in Via Piedigrotta, tel: 081 761 8354. **Europcar**, www.europcar.com Airport, tel: 081 780 5643; Via Santa Lucia, tel: 081 764 9838. **Hertz**, www.hertz.com Airport, tel: 081 780 2971; Via Scarfoglio 11, tel: 081 570 8701; Central Station, Via G. Ricciardi 5, tel: 081 206 228. **Sixt**, www.sixt.com Airport, tel: 081 751 2055, and Via del Poggio 54, tel: 081 743 5320. **Maggiore**, www.maggiore.it Airport, tel: 081 780 3011; Via Cervantes 92, tel: 081 552 1900; Stazione Centrale, Piazza Garibaldi, tel: 081 287 858.

Drive on the right and give way to the left. **Speed limits** for normal cars are 50kph (30mph) in built-up areas, 110kph (70mph) on rural roads, and 130kph (80mph) on motorways. Drinking and driving is strictly forbidden with on-the-spot penalties. There are 24 hour **fuel service stations** at Piazza Carlo III, Via Foria, Piazza Municipio, and Piazza Mergellina. There are **car parks** all around Naples. The Italian website www.parcheggi.it has a map of car parks in the city.

If you are in an **accident**, place a warning triangle 50m (164ft) behind the car and call the police (tel: 112 or 113). Exchange names, addresses and insurance details with other parties and witnesses. Do not admit or imply liability until you have had a chance to think clearly and take advice. If you **breakdown**, tel: 116 and give your location, car registration and make. **The Automobile Club d'Italia** (24-hour emergency, tel: 06 4477, www.aci.it) will come to the rescue. This can be expensive unless you have breakdown cover.

## Money Matters

**Currency:** The currency is the euro (€). It is divided into 100 cents. Notes are available in denominations of €5, €10, €20, €50, €100, €200 and €500, and coins in 1, 2, 5, 10, 20 and 50 euro cents and €1 and €2.

**Credit cards:** All major credit cards are widely accepted.
**Exchange:** Banks tend to cluster in certain areas, such as near Piazza Municipio and behind Via Partenope. Not all have exchange facilities, queues can be long and ID is required for all transactions. Most now have ATM machines that can be used with either a credit card or your normal cheque guarantee card. The exchange booth in the Stazione Centrale stays open daily 07:00 21:00.
**Tipping:** When tipping hotel staff, tip about one euro for the doorman or room service, a couple of euros for the porter, and about the same, per day for the cleaning staff. In restaurants there is usually a 10–15 per cent service charge on the bill, but it is customary to leave a little more small change. For taxis, tip about 10 per cent, and at bars: it is customary to give a small tip, often at the start of the evening, to ensure good service. When at the cinema, give cinema ushers a few coins. Also give a small tip to any custodian who opens a locked area or church for you while you are visiting sights. Tour guides should be given around 5 euros. You can give toilet attendants small coins.

## Children

Children are very welcome everywhere and actually act as an excellent form of introduction to the locals. Take them out to dinner with you in the evening; children under four years get free transport and museum entry and half-price from 4–12 years.

## Disabled Visitors

People are usually willing to help, but most facilities are poor and the area has steep hills and steps, cobbled streets and large areas with no access for cars. It is possible to get around, but will require careful planning. For information try:
**UK: RADAR** (Royal Association for Disability and Rehabilitation), 12 City Forum, 250 City Road, London EC1V 8AF, tel: 020 7250 3222, fax: 020 7250 1212, www.radar.org.uk Tourism for All, c/o Vitalise, Shap Road Industrial Estate, Shap Road, Kendal, Cumbria LA9 6NZ, tel: 0845 124 9971, fax: 01539 735 567, www.tourismforall.org.uk
**USA:** SATH (Society for the Advancement of Travel for the Handicapped), 347 Fifth Ave, Ste 605, New York NY10016, tel: 212 447 7284, fax: 212 447 1928, www.sath.org Mobility International USA, 132 E Broadway, Suite 343, Eugene, Oregon 97401, tel: 541 343 1284, www.muisa.org

## Business Hours

**Banks** open Monday–Friday 08:30–13:00 and again for one hour in the afternoon (usually from 15:00–16:00).
**Post Offices** are open Monday–Saturday, 08:30–19:30; smaller branches usually open Monday–Friday 08:30–17:00 and Saturday 08.30–12:00.
**Shops** are generally open Monday–Saturday, 08:00/09:00–13:00, 16:00–19:00/20:00. More shops are now opening on Sundays. Check the pages of *Qui Napoli* for the opening times of the sights at the time of your visit as they can change with the season and the different churches in the old city, in particular, have some very idiosyncratic hours (best to tackle this area in the morning). Not all rooms in a museum are guaranteed to be open during your visit as staff shortages can sometimes

| CONVERSION CHART | | |
|---|---|---|
| **FROM** | **TO** | **MULTIPLY BY** |
| Millimetres | Inches | 0.0394 |
| Metres | Yards | 1.0936 |
| Metres | Feet | 3.281 |
| Kilometres | Miles | 0.6214 |
| Square kilometres | Square miles | 0.386 |
| Hectares | Acres | 2.471 |
| Litres | Pints | 1.760 |
| Kilograms | Pounds | 2.205 |
| Tonnes | Tons | 0.984 |
| To convert Celsius to Fahrenheit: x 9 ÷ 5 + 32 | | |

## USEFUL PHRASES

Italian pronunciation is logical, but there are a few things to remember. '**C**' is hard (e.g. 'cat') unless followed by an 'I' or 'E', when it becomes 'Ch' (e.g. 'chair'). '**G**' is hard (e.g. 'goat') unless softened by an 'I' or 'E' (e.g. 'gerbil'). '**CC**' is hard (e.g. 'cat') unless followed by an 'I' or an 'E' when it becomes equivalent to the English 'CH' (e.g. 'church'). '**CH**' at the beginning of a word is pronounced as a 'K' (e.g. 'kite').

Good morning/afternoon or evening/night • *Buon giorno/ Buona sera/Buona notte*
Hello/Bye (informal) • *Ciao*
Goodbye • *Arrivaderci*
Yes/No • *Sí/No*
Please • *Per favore*
Thank you (very much) • *Grázie (molte)*
Excuse me • *Mi scusi/prego*
Excuse me (in a crowd) • *Permesso*
You're welcome • *Prego*
Do you speak English? • *Parla inglese?*
I don't understand • *Non ho capito*
I don't know • *No lo so*
I'm sorry • *Mi dispiace*
Gentlemen/Ladies • *Signori/Signore*
Where is... ? • *Dov'è... ?*
When... ? • *Quando ... ?*
What is... ? • *Cos'è... ?*
How much is it? • *Quanto costa?*
Danger • *Pericolo*
Beware • *Attenzione*
No smoking • *Vietato fumare*
Left/right • *A sininstra/A destra*
Entrance/exit • *Entrata/uscita*
Open/closed • *Aperto/chiuso*

mean that individual galleries get closed at random. Tourist Office hours vary, but standard times are Mon–Sat, 09:00–13:00, 16:00–19:00.

## Time Difference

GMT +1 in winter; GMT +2 in summer. The time changes in late March and October.

## Communications

**Stamps** (*francobolli*) are available from hotels, newsagents and tobacconists and post offices. There is usually a small charge for collecting *Poste restante* mail. There are many fax offices and internet cafés. The **telephone** system works well and most international phone cards and 'Country Direct' numbers are recognized. Tariffs are cheapest between 22:00 and 08:00 on weekdays, and all day on Sunday. Public phone boxes use credit cards or phone cards (*schede telefoniche*), sold at newsagents and tobacconists. Coin-operated booths use tokens (*gettoni*). For international calls, look for a phone booth (*telefono a scatti*) in which you can pay for the call at the end. Most people seem to have mobile phones and GSM mobile phones will work (US and Japanese phones may not). For an operator dial 15, for an International operator (Intercontinental) dial 170, for local directory enquiries dial 12. For International directory enquiries dial 176. For reverse charge calls dial 172, followed by the country code. To direct dial abroad 00.

Italy's country code (from abroad) is 39.

## Weights and Measures

Italy uses the metric system.

## Electricity

220V AC, 50 cycles. Most plugs have two round pins; a few have three round pins. Take a travel adapter.

## Personal Safety

Naples has a poor reputation for crime, but it really isn't that bad. Many of the headlines are made by high level corruption and crime which will not affect tourists. There is some petty street crime in certain areas (particularly around the station and the docks). Be careful where you walk alone, especially at night, and watch bags, wallets and phones. It is advisable to keep separate reference copies of all vital documents. There are several different police forces. The **Vigili Urbana** (town police) handle traffic and parking offences in town; the **Polizia Stradale** deal with motorway traffic offences. The **Carabinieri** is responsible for general crime, but thefts should be reported to the **Polizia Statale**. Police headquarters, Via Medina 75, tel: 081 794 1111.

## Emergencies

For general **emergency**, tel: 113. Also call the **police**: 112; **fire**: 115; **ambulance**: 081 752 0696 (24 hours) or 081 752 0850 (daytime only); **car breakdown**: 116; **coast guard**: 081 206 118/9 or 081 206 133/231.